W9-AWH-686

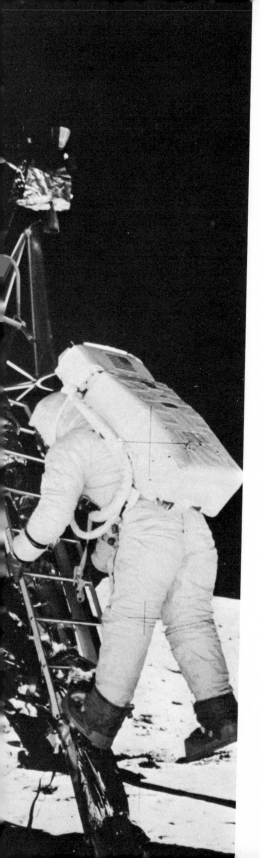

THE MOON
EXPLORERS
TONY SIMON

Illustrated with photographs
Drawings by Lloyd Birmingham

Revised Edition

FOUR WINDS PRESS • NEW YORK

To Ginny and Sue—and the new generation

Acknowledgments

The author wishes to thank the many NASA officials and work crews who took the time at Florida's John F. Kennedy Space Center, Houston's Manned Spacecraft Center, NASA Headquarters in Washington, D.C., and elsewhere, to explain in accurate detail the various operations and objectives for both manned and unmanned missions planned by the United States. The author again extends his deepest appreciation to two NASA astronauts who met with him and inspired him to go ahead with this book, William A. Anders of Apollo 8 and Alan L. Bean of Apollo 12, and is deeply grateful for the cooperation that he received at Houston during the historic Apollo 11 flight.

Tony Simon
New York City
November 1, 1969

Photo Credits
Jacket photos, and pages 1,9,12,20 (bottom), 23,30,
   35,37,41,48,49,59,71,77,83,88,102, and 119, NASA
Frontispiece and pages 53,57,81, and 90, UPI
Pages 20 (top), 43,74, and 93, Wide World
Page 100 (photograph of moon only), Hammond, Inc.
Page 104, adapted from a drawing by Grumman
   Aircraft Engineering Corporation
Page 107, North American Aviation, Inc.
Pages 108 and 123, Grumman Aircraft Engineering
   Corporation

Published by Four Winds Press
A Division of Scholastic Magazines, Inc., New York, N.Y.
Printed in the United States of America
Library of Congress Catalogue Card Number: 78-105331

THIRD PRINTING, 1971

Contents

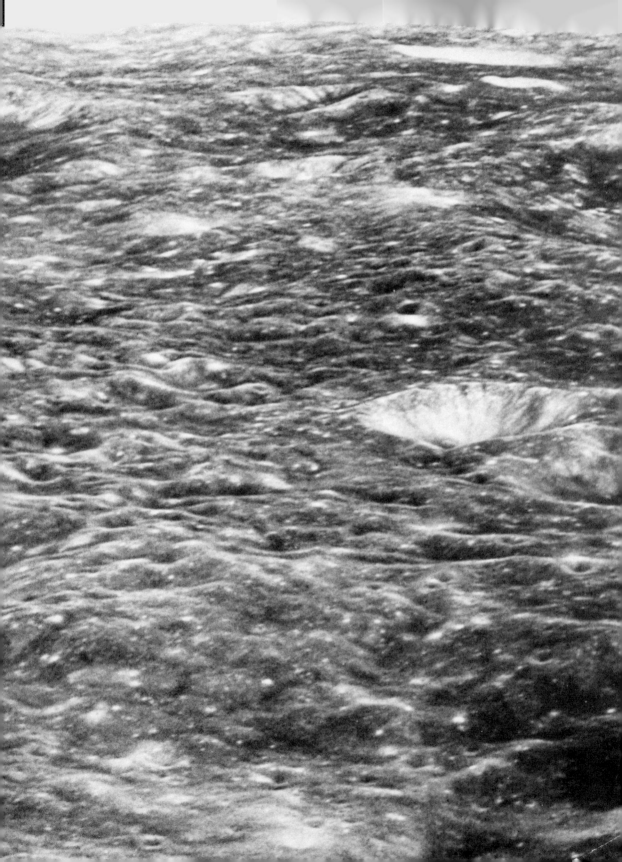

Behind the Moon

SPEEDING THROUGH SPACE, Apollo 8 neared its goal. Straight ahead loomed the moon, only a few thousand miles away. Far behind, nearly 230,000 miles back, lay Earth.

It was Christmas week 1968. . . . For the first time, man was approaching the moon.

Already, Apollo 8 had been three days in flight. With three men aboard, the U.S. spaceship lifted off from Florida early in the morning on December 21. It looped around Earth one-and-one-half times, then headed for the moon.

For the first time, men had soared away from their home planet. For the first time, they had escaped the control of Earth's gravity.

As you know, everything in the universe pulls on

5

Man's first view of the moon's lumpy far side, photographed from Apollo 8. In this close-up, the horizon is about 350 miles away.

everything else. Scientists call this attraction gravity. It is the invisible force that holds the universe together. Gravity holds each of us to Earth . . . it holds the moon to its near-circle path around Earth . . . it holds Earth and all the planets to their orbits around the sun.

By Christmas Eve, Apollo 8 was no longer affected by Earth's gravity, as the control of the moon's gravity grew stronger.

Inside the crowded ship, three U.S. astronauts were at work. The commander was Frank Borman. With him were William A. Anders and James A. Lovell, Jr.

Borman, Lovell, and Anders were a scouting party from Earth to the moon; but they would not make a landing themselves. Their mission: to circle the moon and check out landing sites for the future.

Now the three astronauts were tense and waiting. A major decision was about to be radioed to Apollo 8, deep in space, from mission control in Houston, Texas. Within minutes, the astronauts would be ordered to guide Apollo 8 into one of two courses:

Fire a rocket to slow the spaceship, go into moon orbit, and fly 10 times around the moon.

Or . . .

Make no change in the ship's speed, fly behind the moon just *once*, then head for home — with most of the scouting mission undone.

Why might mission control cut the flight short?

Putting Apollo 8 into moon orbit was risky. Everything would have to work just right. Suppose the ship could not get up enough speed later to escape the moon's gravity?

It would be trapped in moon orbit. It could never return to Earth. If the scientists at mission control thought there was a chance Apollo 8 would not work properly in moon orbit, they would call off all plans and order Apollo 8 back to Earth.

A voice from mission control broke the silence.

"This is Houston at 68:04 (68 hours, four minutes after lift-off). You are go for LOI (lunar orbit insertion)."

Apollo 8 was working perfectly. They were cleared for the first of the 10 trips around the moon.

"O.K., Apollo 8 is go," Commander Borman radioed back.

The spaceship sped on, and the bright white moon grew larger and larger.

Houston called in again. "You are riding the best bird we can find. Two minutes and 50 seconds away from time of loss of signal. . . . We'll see you on the other side. . . . One minute until loss of signal. . . . All systems go. . . . Safe journey, guys."

Anders answered with a cheery, "Thanks a lot, troops. We'll see you on the other side."

Borman said, "Roger" — and then all was silence, a sudden and scary kind of silence.

All radio contact between Apollo 8 and Earth had ended. The ship was behind the moon.

A "Moon" of the Moon

Soon Borman pushed a button that set off a mighty braking rocket. It burned violently for four minutes and cut Apollo 8's speed from 5,700 to 3,600 miles an hour.

Moving in to 70 miles from the surface, the ship started its first trip around Earth's satellite. In fact, the ship now became a captured "moon" of the moon.

Minutes ticked by. The silence stretched out. On Earth the suspense mounted, along with gnawing concern for the crew's safety. Then, within an hour, Apollo 8 came out from behind the moon.

"We've got it! We've got it!" shouted a voice in mission control. "Apollo 8 is in lunar orbit."

"Good to hear your voice," said Lovell, as contact again was made with Earth. For the next few minutes, the crew reported on the ship's performance and instruments, and on conditions inside Apollo 8. All was well.

Then Lovell reported one of man's first impressions of the moon close up:

"The moon is essentially gray. No color. Looks like plaster of Paris or sort of grayish deep sand. We can see quite a bit of detail. . . . The craters are all rounded off."

From early morning Christmas Eve until early morning Christmas Day 1968, Apollo 8 circled the moon. Nearly all of the moon's far side was in sunlight, giving a clear view of moon features never before seen directly by man.

During the 10 orbits, the men took still photos and color and black-and-white movies of the moon. They sent live TV pictures back to Earth. And they picked out landmarks and landing sites for future manned flights.

"The moon is a different thing to each of us," said Borman. "My own impression is that it's a vast, lonely,

The Apollo 8 astronauts: left to right, James A. Lovell, Jr., William A. Anders, and Frank Borman.

forbidding-type of existence — a great expanse of nothing that looks rather like clouds and clouds of pumice stone. It certainly would not appear to be a very inviting place to live or work."

Lovell agreed. "It makes you realize just what you have back on Earth. The Earth from here is a vast oasis in the emptiness of space."

Anders said: "The horizon is very stark. The sky is pitch black and the moon is quite light. The contrast between the sky and the moon is a vivid dark line."

Once, during an early orbit, Houston radioed: "There's a beautiful moon out there tonight."

And Borman, looking at a bright blue Earth laced with white clouds, answered: "We were just saying, 'That's a beautiful Earth back there.'"

The view of Earth in the deep loneliness of space moved Lovell. "I keep imagining I am some lonely traveler from another planet," he said. "What should I think about the earth at this altitude? Whether it should be inhabited or not."

9

Back to Earth

After nearly 20 hours of moon-orbiting, the time had come to restart the rocket engine and head back to Earth. Now the ship's speed had to increase from 3,600 miles an hour to nearly 6,000 miles an hour. Houston came in with a brief radio message: "All systems are go, Apollo 8."

"Roger," answered Borman.

Then, for the 10th time, Apollo 8 disappeared behind the moon — and into bleak silence.

Again the world waited. Again time ticked off slowly as Apollo 8 moved across the far side of the moon.

On Earth millions wondered and worried about the next few minutes of the flight. Would the rocket engine go off? Would the ship's added speed break the grip of the moon's gravity?

Aboard Apollo 8 the three astronauts were calm, confident that the rocket engine would fire perfectly.

And it did — at the end of the 10th orbit, just as the ship came over the moon's horizon.

Now, "climbing spectacularly," in Borman's words, Apollo 8 shot away from the moon.

As the pioneer ship escaped the moon's gravity and headed for home, a relieved Lovell radioed this message: "Please be informed that there *is* a Santa Claus!"

Back toward Earth sped Apollo 8. But danger lay ahead at the very end of the half-million-mile round trip. The astronauts still had to re-enter the Earth's atmosphere — and at just the right angle.

Imagine that Apollo 8 came in too steeply. It might break apart or burn up from the terrible friction of Earth's atmosphere.

10

Imagine that it came in at too shallow an angle. It might "bounce off" the atmosphere like a tossed rock skimming across a lake. The ship would miss Earth entirely. It would go into a far-ranging orbit around Earth. Then, before Apollo 8 could come around again to land, the men would run out of oxygen.

Hour after hour passed. Mile after mile vanished. Nearer and nearer to Earth sped Apollo 8. "We're happy to report that the Earth is getting larger," radioed Borman.

As the ship shot along, pulled in faster and faster by Earth's gravity, its speed built up. It jumped to 24,700 miles an hour, a new record for man — *10 times faster than the speed of a bullet fired from a powerful rifle.*

At this tremendous speed, Apollo 8 re-entered Earth's atmosphere on December 27, 1968. The angle of entry was perfect — not too shallow, not too steep. Down toward the Pacific Ocean came the ship. Two parachutes opened out to help slow Apollo 8, then three big chutes opened to ease it into the ocean.

The astronauts had "threaded a needle." The aim of the returning Apollo was so exact that it splashed down only 5,000 yards from the carrier *Yorktown*, the recovery ship. The feat was especially risky because Apollo 8 was the first spaceship to land in complete darkness. As the sun came up about an hour later, each man was lifted aboard the *Yorktown* — safe and sound.

America's daring explorers were home again from man's first voyage around the moon.

Borman, Lovell, and Anders had joined such great explorers of history as Columbus, Magellan, and Cabot.

The Meaning of Apollo 8

Apollo 8 scored many firsts. For the first time
- man himself had escaped the control of Earth's gravity — traveling 230,000 miles into space.
- man himself had traveled around the moon and seen its far side with his own eyes.
- man had safely re-entered Earth's atmosphere from outer space.
- man had moved at such great speed — 24,700 miles an hour.

In this drawing, three giant parachutes ease the splashdown of an Apollo command module. Recovery helicopters hover overhead.

Apollo 8's mission was to serve as a rehearsal and scouting party for moon explorers to come. It had been a tremendous success.

Soon man would land on the moon and take the first steps across its surface. Soon he would learn more than he had ever known about the moon. Soon he might find answers to such questions as:

When was the moon formed?

What is it made of?

Where did it come from?

Is there life on the moon?

Was there *ever* life on the moon?

How were its thousands of craters formed?

Did the moon ever have real seas that dried up, or an atmosphere that drifted away?

And most important of all: Can the moon help man solve the mystery of how Earth and its sister planets were formed? Does the moon bear clues to the beginnings of life — on Earth?

The Moon — What's It Like?

THE APOLLO 8 ASTRONAUTS were the first men to see the moon's far side. Only 70 miles up, they had an excellent view.

"The back of the moon looks like a battlefield," said Anders, during one of their 45-minute passes across the moon's far side. "It has hole upon hole, and crater upon crater. It looks like a dirty beach, grayish white, and churned up, like the sand of a volleyball court on a beach. The back of the moon is all beat up, a lot of holes and bumps."

Unlike astronauts, we see only one side of the moon — the side that always faces Earth. Several American and Russian *unmanned* spacecraft have gone behind the moon and sent back photographs. But until Apollo 8, no man had ever seen the far side of the moon with his own eyes.

Yet the moon turns and moves. It spins on its own axis, making a full turn as it revolves around Earth.

Why then do we see only one side of the moon? Why is the other side always turned away from Earth? Let's act out the answer:

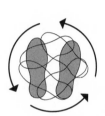 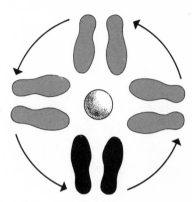

1. Stand in the center of a room. Spin slowly until you have made one full turn. (As you spin, you will face each wall.) When you have made one full turn, stop. You have *rotated*, or turned, completely around yourself.

2. Put a ball on the floor. Pretend that the ball is Earth and you are the moon. Take short steps, sideways, around the ball. Keep your toes pointed toward it. Stop when you have come back to your starting point. You again have *rotated* once around yourself, just as you did in number 1 above. (While turning, you again faced each wall.) But this time you also have *revolved* once around the ball.

Notice that the front of your body always faced the ball. Your back never did. In much this way, the moon *rotates* (spins around) once — during the same time that it *revolves* once around Earth. That is why we never see the far side of the moon from Earth.

The Apollo 8 astronauts were the first men to get around the problem — and the moon! From them we learned that its far side "is more ravaged" (torn up) than its near side. Yet in some ways, the far side is much like the near side.

Both sides are rocky, rugged, barren, silent, hostile.

Both have dust, tan sandy soil, pebbles, gray lowlands, plains, hills, mountains.

Both have strangely-winding narrow valleys and arrow-straight long valleys.

What's more, both sides are badly pock-marked with craters (holes). These craters range in size from several inches to 175-or-more miles across.

Our Closest Neighbor

The moon is our closest neighbor in space. As it revolves in its near circle path around Earth, the nearest it comes to us is about 220,000 miles. The farthest it gets from us is about 250,000 miles. It takes the moon about 27 days to make its full orbit around Earth.

The moon shines — but not by its own light. Like Earth, it reflects the sun's light. During its 27-day orbit, the side of the moon we see from Earth turns slowly toward the sun, then away from it. As it turns gradually toward the sun, we begin to see what looks like a quarter slice of

16

the moon. When the sun is shining fully on the side near Earth, we see a full moon. Then, as the Earth-side of the moon turns slowly away from the sun, it seems to be growing smaller again. Finally it seems to disappear completely. (The sun is then shining on the far side of the moon.)

As moons go, ours is a big one. Many planets have moons, but ours is the biggest compared to its "mother" planet. Our moon has 12 million square miles of surface (roughly as much as Africa).

Although big for a moon, our moon is much smaller than Earth. The moon's diameter is 2,160 miles — or about one fourth of Earth's diameter of 7,900 miles. It would take about 50 moons to fill a hollow Earth.

Because the moon is smaller than Earth, its pull is weaker. The moon's gravity is one sixth of Earth's. So things weigh less on the moon.

An astronaut who weighed 180 pounds here would weigh 30 pounds on the moon. He could jump six times as high as on Earth. He could throw a ball six times higher. He could lift things that would be much too heavy on Earth. A rock that weighs 600 pounds on Earth weighs about 100 pounds on the moon. A man could move much faster on the moon than on Earth. But he might also have a harder time stopping. And he might feel, as he bounced along on foot, that he was about to rise and soar away like a kite.

What Scientists Wonder About the Moon

Scientists believe that both the moon and Earth — in fact the whole solar system — are about four-and-half billion years old. Some say the moon and Earth were formed the same way at the same time. If so, the moon may give clues to Earth's early history. This is why:

The rocks and soil from Earth's first billion-or-so years have completely worn away and changed. This erosion was caused by air, wind, water, ice. Lost forever were clues to how Earth was formed.

This does not seem to have happened on the moon. It probably had no air, wind, surface water, or weather. The moon's surface does not seem to have undergone weather erosion. Most of the surface probably has not been greatly changed for billions of years. By studying moon rocks, on and below the surface and in the highlands, scientists may learn secrets of the moon's beginnings — and in turn much about Earth's "missing" billion years.

So for scientists, rock collecting loomed as a key job of the Apollo moon explorers.

In the early 1960's, scientists wondered whether or not a spaceship could land safely on the moon. Some scientists believed that the surface of the moon was a powdery sand, deep enough to swallow a landing spaceship.

Then Russian and American instrument ships landed on the moon. U.S. Surveyors, for example, ripped their robot claws into the surface, but did not sink. The sandlike layer seemed to be only inches deep. Below it seemed to be solid rock. The surface was definitely strong enough to hold a spaceship. Astronauts could walk on the moon safely.

But when the Apollo 8 crew made the first manned orbits around the moon, they made a new discovery that alarmed scientists preparing for the future moon landing. Beneath its sandy surface, the moon was "lumpy."

Some scientists, describing the lumpiness of the moon, say it is like a giant raisin cake. The raisins are iron or volcanic *masses* — *con*centrations or huge chunks buried under the surface. Scientists call them *mascons*. They make the pull of gravity uneven across the surface.

The Apollo scientists were afraid that as landing astronauts passed over a mascon, its stronger gravity would give a sudden pull on the spaceship. The ship would wobble downward 30 feet or more. For the moment, the spaceship might be hard to control.

Mascons may be signs that the moon once had surface water. They are usually found in the moon's dark areas called mares, or seas, though they are waterless. At one time, fast flowing rivers may have carried iron and other heavy elements into moon oceans. After millions of years, the oceans dried up into vast cracked plains, but the iron and other heavy sediments collected there remained. Other scientists believe there was never that much water on the moon. They think mascons may simply be meteorites (flying rocks from space) which have drilled themselves deep into the surface, or that mascons may be the results of volcanic action.

Scientists hoped that when moon explorers gathered up samples of soil from one of the mares, clues about mascons would be provided.

Another moon mystery scientists want to solve is how the millions of craters that pepper both sides of the moon were formed.

Again, scientists disagree among themselves. Some say craters were the result of active volcanoes working in either of two ways: A crater may have been formed when a volcano erupted violently. Or, volcanic rock, bubbling upward from below, may have just pushed against the surface and formed a big "blister." Later, the blister "popped" or cooled, and the ground above it caved in and formed a crater.

Other scientists do not believe the craters were formed by volcanic action. They say the craters were probably formed by meteorites crashing into the moon. Earth is protected from these flying rocks, because the friction of

Top: Part of the moon's near side. Long ago, Galileo thought the big, dark, smooth areas looked like oceans and named them mares, or seas. Bottom: Part of the moon's far side. There are few mares on the far side. Scientists wonder why the two sides are different.

our atmosphere burns up most of them before they can hit the surface. But the moon has no atmosphere for protection. It has been pounded by millions of meteorites, large and small, smashing into it at more than 30 miles a second — crashing with the force of atom bombs.

Many scientists believe that both theories are possible, and that moon craters probably were formed both by volcanic action and by meteorites.

Apollo 8's moon voyagers didn't settle the question. "There are an awful lot of holes on the moon," they reported. "There are enough for both ideas."

Only astronauts setting foot on the moon would be able to help scientists answer the crater questions.

Scientists also want to know if the moon is "alive" or "dead" — whether it is cold and inactive, or whether it once had a hot, molten core like Earth's — and whether it still has one today. And are volcanoes active on the moon? The volcano question, like the crater question, causes arguments among scientists.

Most scientists agree that the moon shows much evidence of lava outpourings from volcanoes. Some believe if it ever was hot it could not have cooled off in four-and-a-half billion years. They say the moon may have active volcanoes and other hot spots, and that it was — and still is — hot deep under its surface. Recent instrument readings and telescope sightings support this view. Hints of hot spots have been found here and there on the moon, especially in some large craters. Other observers have seen glowing red spots and flashes of light on the moon.

Craters pepper both sides of the moon. "Were they all formed by meteorites, or are some volcanic?" scientists ask. The biggest of the craters shown, photographed from Apollo 8, is 40 miles across.

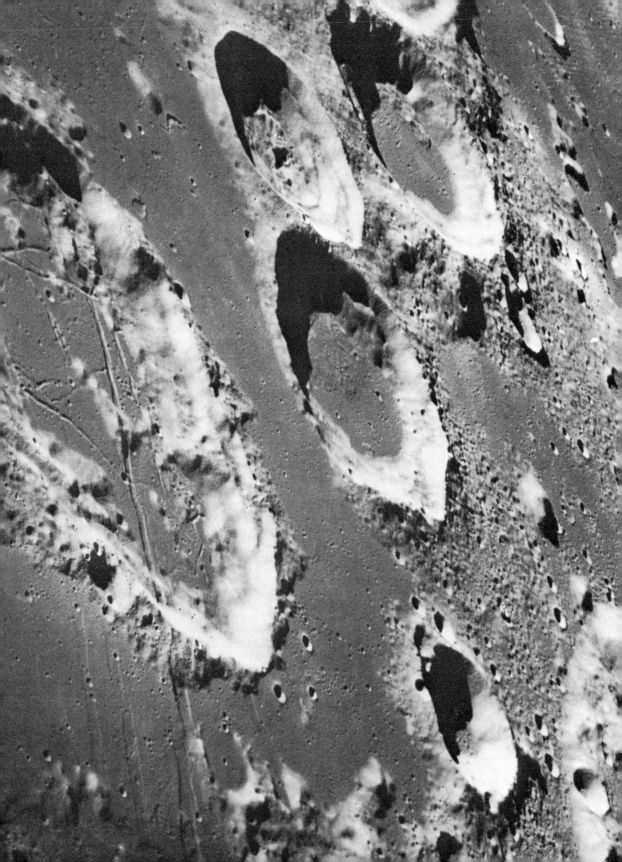

From Apollo 8, Lovell reported seeing a swirling pattern inside some craters. The swirls are somewhat like those made by lava flows on Earth. Anders said that much of the moon's surface appeared to show evidence of past volcanoes.

About volcanoes, too, scientists waited eagerly for the information the first moon-walkers would provide.

Life on the Moon?

From Apollo 8 we heard again what we had long known:

"The moon certainly would not appear to be a very inviting place to live or work," said Commander Borman.

Without a spacesuit, no man could live more than a few moments on the moon. There is no food or water on the surface. There is no air — and therefore no wind, no clouds, no rain, and no protection from the sun's death-dealing radiation or from crashing meteorites. Men could not breathe. And they could not hear each other speak, because sound waves must be carried by air. With no air to reduce the sun's heat or spread it out evenly, temperatures climb to 250 degrees Fahrenheit during the blazing two-week day. Without protection, a man's blood would boil and bubble. The two-week night comes suddenly, with temperatures falling quickly to 250 degrees below zero Fahrenheit. A man without a spacesuit would turn to solid ice.

So there is no life on the surface of the moon — not as we know life. Unaided, Earth life could not survive on the moon.

"The moon is the kind of place where you would put things to sterilize them," commented a U.S. scientist.

This doesn't mean that there *never* was life on the moon — or that some kind of simple, microscopic life does not now exist in the cracks below the surface where there may be traces of water. But the chances for even this kind of simple life are very thin.

The first men to land on the moon were almost sure to find there an empty, dead world.

Why Go to the Moon?

If it is such a harsh horror of a place to visit, then why does man want to go to the moon?

It moves him. It dares him. It fascinates him. It stirs his imagination. It flames his desire to know everything about the solar system — about the universe! With the moon as his base, man could learn more about Earth and also see more clearly into deep space. He could soar out farther. He could learn more.

"Man must know," say scientists. "He is a thinking creature, a creature who can never stop thinking."

Because man thinks, he finds ways to learn what he wants to know. Man's thinking made the mighty moon rocket, the marvelous spaceship, and the delicate moon-landing bug.

Reaching for the Moon

YES, MAN IS a thinker. And a man who thought deeply launched the U.S. program to put men on the moon. He was President John F. Kennedy.

In 1961 President Kennedy, in a speech before Congress, told Americans:

"I believe this nation should commit itself to achieving the goal, before this decade is out, of landing a man on the moon and returning him safely to Earth. . . . In a very real sense, it will not be one man going to the moon, it will be an entire nation."

President Kennedy spoke one month after a spectacular flight had thrilled the world. In April 1961, Yuri A. Gagarin of Russia had orbited Earth to become man's first space traveler. Later, in August 1961, Gherman S. Titov of Russia orbited Earth 17 times and landed safely.

Now, Americans, too, began reaching for the moon. Many took up their young President's challenge and got behind him with a will. The nation supported what was to be a 24-billion-dollar space project. In time, 400,000 Americans would take part, the greatest peacetime teamwork effort any nation had ever achieved.

The project called for muscle power and brain power. U.S. industries joined in and in time 20,000 companies took part, building rockets, launch pads, space capsules, instruments, space labs, and tracking stations.

The U.S. trained astronauts, scientists, engineers, technicians. NASA, the National Aeronautics and Space Administration, began to work out the program for reaching the moon.

At first there were disappointments and mistakes. Schedules fell behind. Plans did not hold up. Rockets exploded on launch pads. But the U.S. went ahead with tests of one-man, two-man, and three-man spacecraft.

Project Mercury

The first step toward a moon landing came in 1961 with Project Mercury, the one-man space flights, designed to test whether men could live and work in space. The first American in space was Alan B. Shepard, Jr. In May 1961, he lifted off from Florida and flew 116 miles above Earth. He came down in the Atlantic Ocean, 300 miles from Florida, after a 15-minute ride.

The first American to orbit Earth was John H. Glenn, Jr., in 1962. In the space capsule Friendship 7, he orbited Earth three times during an 81,000-mile flight that lasted five hours.

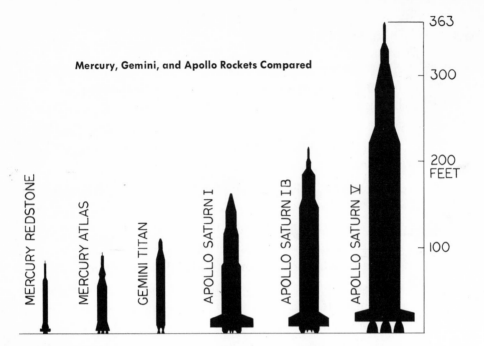

Mercury, Gemini, and Apollo Rockets Compared

MERCURY REDSTONE
MERCURY ATLAS
GEMINI TITAN
APOLLO SATURN I
APOLLO SATURN I B
APOLLO SATURN V

363
300
200 FEET
100

Like Shepard, Glenn was weightless — a new experience in those days. With amusement, Glenn described what happened when he and his camera became weightless.

"I had this little hand camera, and I had taken a picture, and I wanted to do something with a switch immediately. And it just seemed natural . . . rather than put the camera away, to just put it out in mid-air and let go of it. . . . I put on the switch and reached back for the camera and went on with the work."

Project Gemini

After Mercury came the two-man flights of Project Gemini. They checked equipment, instruments, and space techniques that would one day be used in moon

28

flight. It was the Gemini astronauts who tested the art of docking, or connecting, two space capsules in orbit.

During the Gemini 4 flight in June 1965, Edward H. White left the capsule and floated about outside for 23 minutes — the first U.S. astronaut to take a "walk in space."

But the U.S. was still behind the Soviet Union in space advances. Aleksei A. Leonov, a Russian, had taken man's first space walk a few months before White.

Project Apollo

Apollo flights were under way by the middle of 1965. The idea behind Apollo was:

• Build a rocket powerful enough to break away from Earth's gravity.

• Build a moonship (command and service module) big and sturdy enough to carry three men to moon orbit.

• Build a smaller craft (the lunar module) that would separate from the moonship, land two men on the moon, then bring them back to the moonship.

The most difficult part of the Apollo flight would be maneuvering the lunar module, or LM (pronounced "lem"). Testing LM would be so complex that it was saved for last. The early Apollo flights tested only the command and service modules — unmanned — and the booster rockets. The testing moved along well, and the first manned flight was set for February 1967.

Then tragedy struck.

A few days before the scheduled manned flight, Apollo was poised, pointing skyward, on its launch pad. Inside

The astronauts who died in 1967 Apollo fire: left to right, Edward H. White, Virgil I. Grissom, and Roger B. Chaffee.

the sealed ship was the three-man crew. The astronauts were looking over their instruments and conducting routine tests. Suddenly fire broke out inside the ship. The blaze spread within seconds. The men died only minutes before they could be pulled out.

The nation mourned the loss of astronauts Virgil I. (Gus) Grissom, Edward H. White, and Roger B. Chaffee. The accident was a shocking reminder of the dangers astronauts face. The space program had been going so smoothly, people had begun to forget that things could go wrong in a spaceship with more than 200,000 moving parts.

The fire set back manned Apollo flights for months. Great pains were now taken to check out every part for still more safety. Slowly, the picture brightened again.

Late in 1967, Apollo 4 made an eight-and-one-half-hour flight. There was no crew this time, but it marked a step forward. For the first time, the mighty Saturn V rocket (not the smaller boosters used until then) roared into space, reaching a top speed of 25,000 miles an hour.

This flight proved that the three-stage rocket could lift off and fly. It showed that the engines could refire in space for added speed or to correct flight positions. And when the ship streaked back white hot — at seven miles a second — from an altitude of 11,200 miles, it was clear that the Apollo heat shield could stand up under temperatures of 5,000 degrees Fahrenheit.

Apollo had the rocket — and the thrust — needed to reach the moon. Once more, the U.S. had the confidence and the will to get there.

But two more unmanned tests lay ahead before NASA would try another flight with a crew:

Apollo 5 tested LM in space for the first time. Without a crew, the moon-landing bug worked perfectly.

Apollo 6 fired a dummy, unmanned moonship atop a Saturn V rocket deep into space. The return drop again tested the heat shield. Though the shield was blackened and blistered by the extreme temperature, it had protected the ship. It would protect men, too.

The time was now at hand for the first Apollo test with a crew aboard since the tragic fire.

In the fall of 1968, Apollo 7, riding a Saturn IB rocket, lifted off. Walter M. Schirra, Jr., Walter Cunningham, and Donn F. Eisele orbited Earth 163 times in 11 days. The astronauts traveled four-and-a-half million miles at a top speed of 17,500 miles an hour.

It was the first successful manned flight of Apollo — the mission that would land explorers on the moon.

Two months later (as you read in chapter one) Apollo 8 made its Christmas 1968 flight to the moon, orbiting it

10 times and photographing its far side.

Early in 1969, Apollo 9 gave LM its first manned test.

The Apollo 9 crew: James A. McDivitt, David R. Scott, and Russell L. Schweickart. The code name for the command ship was *Gumdrop;* for LM, *Spider.* During the Apollo 9 mission, McDivitt and Schweickart flew in LM while Scott piloted the command ship alone.

McDivitt and Schweickart tested LM's spidery legs to see if they opened out properly. They did. They also checked out LM's electrical system, its computer system, its rocket engines. For six hours, circling 135 miles above Earth, they flew in LM. At times they were more than 110 miles away from — and out of sight of — the command ship.

At one point Schweickart tested the "portable life-support system" (PLSS). PLSS is a 125-pound back pack, almost as big as a suitcase. It supplies oxygen for breathing and helps keep an astronaut cool. It was designed for use by men on the moon or on space walks. Without it, a man would not live long in either place.

To test the pack, Schweickart left LM for a 40-minute space walk. He showed that men could, in an emergency, move from LM to the command ship through space.

Later, LM and the Apollo 9 command ship joined together. All three men then returned home safely. LM had done well during its 10-day test in Earth-orbit — within Earth's gravity. One question remained: Would LM work as well within moon gravity?

The answer came with Apollo 10 and astronauts Thomas P. Stafford, John W. Young, and Eugene A. Cernan.

The second ship to escape the control of Earth's gravity, Apollo 10, flew to within 67 miles of the moon's surface in May 1969. Then, as in Apollo 9, two men — Stafford and Cernan — crawled into LM from the command ship.

LM, code-named *Snoopy*, moved to only nine miles from the moon's surface. Then it returned Stafford and Cernan to the orbiting command ship, code-named *Charlie Brown*. It was a dress-rehearsal of the moon-landing — except for the landing.

LM and the command ship docked above the moon's surface. Both flew around the moon together 31 times; then the three astronauts took a quarter-of-a-million-mile ride home and splashed down safely.

Apollo 10 had been a huge success. Apollo had now been tested as much as it could be. The stage was set for the first manned landing on the moon.

American astronauts had come a long way since President Kennedy's challenge to the nation in 1961.

A Rocket, a Moonship, a Bug

EVEN WHILE APOLLO 10 circled the moon, Apollo 11 was inching along toward its launching pad.

The time: 12:30 p.m., May 20, 1960 — nearly two months before lift-off.

The place: John F. Kennedy Space Center, Florida.

The scene: Bright sunlight splattered over Florida sand, palm trees, lakes, and marshland. In a corner of this flat area loomed a huge building. Fifty-two stories high, 716 feet long, 518 feet wide, it had more room inside than any other building in the world. It was the Vertical Assembly Building. Here Apollo 11 and Saturn V had been put together in lift-off position.

Two giant doors swung open. Out moved a steel crawler-transporter on tank-like treads — a platform as big as a baseball infield. Standing upright, outlined

34

John F. Kennedy Space Center, Florida: Dwarfing nearby cars, Apollo 11/Saturn V rides a huge transporter toward launch pad 39A.

against the sky, Apollo/Saturn towered over the platform.

The huge transporter crept down a three-and-one-half-mile-long road, moving just one mile every two hours, gently and carefully so the giant spaceship would not topple over. Finally it came to a stop at a launch pad.

From here, Pad 39A, Apollo 11 would begin man's most spectacular voyage.

A Look at Apollo 11

Let's have a closer look at an Apollo spaceship.

Apollo 11/Saturn V stood 363 feet tall, or higher than a 36-story skyscraper. Actually, it was eight ships in one. Each could fly on its own.

• Three "ships" were the stages of the Saturn V rocket, one on top of the other. (Astronauts called Saturn V "the stack.") Each would fire, then drop off as the next stage took over.

• A fourth ship was the escape tower.

• A fifth was the combined command and service modules.

• A sixth was the lower half of LM. Its rocket engine would move LM away from the command/service ship and down to the moon's surface.

• A seventh was the upper half of LM. Its rocket engine would lift it off the moon and back to the orbiting command/service ship.

• And finally, there was the command module. It also would fly alone, after LM and the service module were rocketed away. At the very end of the trip the command module would re-enter Earth's atmosphere alone.

36

A breakdown of an Apollo/Saturn V spacecraft. Eight of the sections or combinations of sections are able to fly on their own.

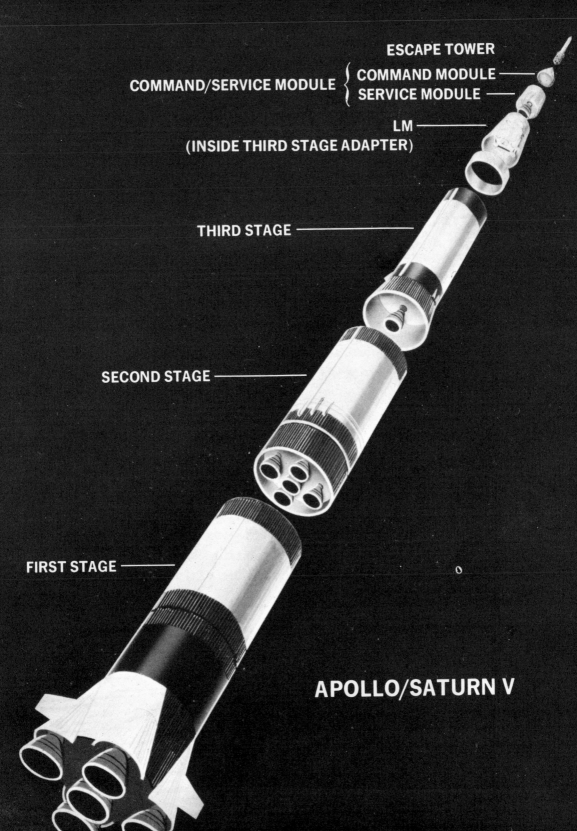

ESCAPE TOWER

COMMAND/SERVICE MODULE { COMMAND MODULE
                         SERVICE MODULE

LM
(INSIDE THIRD STAGE ADAPTER)

THIRD STAGE

SECOND STAGE

FIRST STAGE

APOLLO/SATURN V

Saturn V: A Mighty Rocket

Saturn V, the rocket, was 281 feet tall. Each of its three stages was a rocket.

As you know, a rocket works much like a toy balloon. What happens when you let go of an air-filled balloon? The air rushes out. As the air escapes in one direction, the balloon spurts ahead in the opposite direction. In a rocket, heated gases rush out of the back of the rocket. This creates a "reaction force" — a thrust. The rocket is thrust forward. The faster gas flows through the rocket, the greater is the thrust forward.

Engineers measure thrust in pounds. To lift a rocket off the ground, the number of pounds of thrust must be more than the number of pounds the rocket weighs.

"It's like a tug-of-war between Earth's gravity and the rocket engine's thrust," engineers explain. "If the engine can push itself *up* more forcefully than gravity pulls it *down*, the rocket will rise. The greater the thrust is — over the rocket's weight — the faster the rocket takes off."

Saturn V had three stages. This is why:

An Apollo spaceship had to escape Earth's gravity to lift off. No single U.S. rocket was able to do this — *and* provide enough thrust to move Apollo all the way to the moon. It would take three rockets to do the job.

Once a rocket stage fired and burned out, it was dead weight and would be dropped.

In Saturn V's *first stage alone*, a cluster of five engines would burn more than four million pounds of fuel and produce a thrust of seven-and-a-half million pounds. That was *equal to all the horsepower in a row of cars, bumper to bumper, from Los Angeles to New York.*

The first stage would lift Apollo 40 miles into space, then be blown off and fall into the Atlantic Ocean.

The second stage would take over with its cluster of five engines and a thrust of one million pounds. It too would burn itself out and be blown into the Atlantic.

The third-stage rocket would put Apollo into a "parking orbit" about 115 miles above the Earth. The third stage would stay with the ship longer than the first two. Later, its 200,000-pound-thrust engine would fire again to start Apollo out of Earth orbit and toward the moon. Then it too would separate from Apollo; but instead of falling back to Earth, the third stage would curve around the moon and go into orbit around the sun.

On the launch pad, Apollo/Saturn weighed six-and-a half million pounds — but would lose weight quickly after lift-off. Apollo 10, for example, burned fuel at the rate of 830,000 pounds a second. At the end of its moon trip, after burning fuel and dropping off rocket stages and other parts, only the command module was left. Apollo 10 was down to a mere 13,000 pounds.

The Moonship: A Home in Space

The Apollo 11 moonship was made up of the command module, the service module, and LM.

Above the command module was an escape tower, a 30-foot-tall needle-shaped structure. If something were to go wrong in the first two-and-a-half minutes after lift-off, the four-ton escape tower would lift the command module and the crew away from the rest of Apollo and drop them to safety by parachute. After these minutes, escape no longer possible, the tower would be dropped.

Below the escape tower was the six-ton, cone-shaped command module, the only section that would come back to Earth. It was 10 feet high and 13 feet across. It had five windows, an instrument panel, a computer, radios, TV cameras. Also packed in the command module were parachutes, food, rocket engines, 15 miles of wiring, and two million separate parts (mostly small transistors).

For the astronauts, the command module would be home during a flight. At lift-off, the men would be on their backs, strapped to their couch seats. Later, weightless, they could move around a little in the cabin.

The command module was small, no bigger than a walk-in closet. But it was comfortable. It was air conditioned to keep temperatures at around 75 degrees Fahrenheit. It had a steady supply of fresh air — pure oxygen, in fact. It was a cockpit, bedroom, radio and TV studio, office, laboratory, bathroom, kitchen — all in one. The men would work in their flight overalls at different intrument panels lining the wall. They would sleep on their couches or in sleeping bags stored underneath.

Below the command module was the 25-ton service module. It held the fuel, water, and gases needed during a flight. It stored equipment for producing electric power. And it had its own rocket engine for making mid-course corrections. The service module engine also provided the extra thrust Apollo would need to get back home.

In an early model of the command module, three men show how astronauts can work and sleep in a space the size of a walk-in closet.

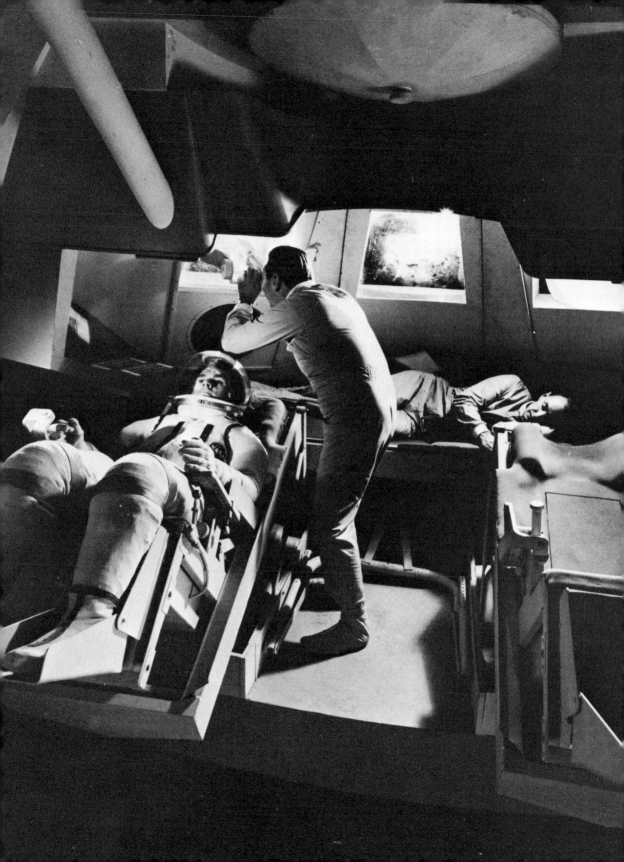

LM: The Space Bug

LM looked like a strange bug.

Its "mouth" was an opening for entering and leaving. Its "eyes" were two windows. It had four 12-foot-long spidery-looking legs. Its saucer-like "feet" were landing pods. And like a bug, it too had "feelers" — antennas and rocket clusters that stuck out from all sides. Unlike a bug, LM weighed 16 tons and was 23 feet tall and 31 feet wide. Yet its code name of *Spider* on the Apollo 9 flight was most fitting.

On the Apollo 9 mission a manned LM went out into space on its own for the first time. When it returned to the command ship, astronaut David Scott, watching it approach, said, "You're the biggest, friendliest, funniest looking spider I've ever seen."

LM was built to do one job: get two Apollo astronauts from the command ship to the moon, and from the moon back to the command ship.

Both men would work side by side, 44 inches apart, standing up. They would face two triangle-shaped windows, slanted forward and down so they could see what was ahead and below. A big panel at LM's front center would let both men share certain controls. Each would have a set of hand controls. With these, either man could move LM in any direction, even inches at a time.

LM had 18 rockets, 40 miles of wiring, eight different radio systems, six antennas, radar equipment, and a computer system. The inside of LM had no rough surface or sharp piece of equipment sticking out. This is why:

On the moon, an astronaut would wear a sealed spacesuit filled with pure oxygen. The suit would keep his

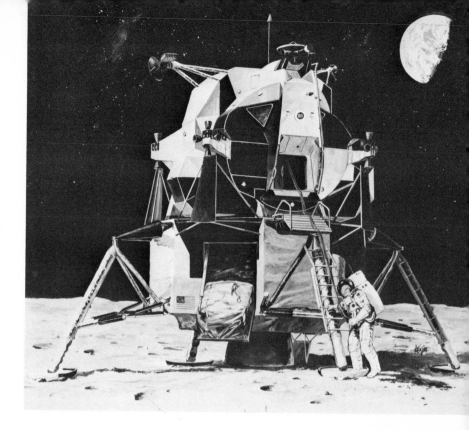

An astronaut steps onto the moon from LM, which looks like a giant bug. In this drawing, Earth shines in the black lunar sky.

body at the same temperature and under the same pressure as on Earth. Suppose he were to rip his suit on a sharp edge in LM? The oxygen might leak from the suit while he was on the moon. If this happened, he would die.

Something else LM did not have was a seat. This saved space. The men would be weightless in LM until the braking rockets fired for landing. They could float in a sitting or a napping position and rest without anything to support them. Or they could sleep on the floor or on the engine cover. Anyway, the ride in LM between Apollo and the moon would be short.

LM was designed to fly only outside Earth's atmosphere. It was the first true "space" ship, for it was built *only* for flight in space. Its paper-thin aluminum sides would be burned up flying through Earth's atmosphere. Its landing ladder could never be used on Earth. The ladder might break if a man pressed down on it with his six-times-greater Earth weight.

During the beginning of a moon flight, LM would be folded snugly inside Saturn V's third stage, between the rocket and the command/service modules. This would protect LM from the friction of Earth's atmosphere as Apollo headed out for the moon. Once away from Earth, the command/service ship would pull away from the third stage rocket and LM. It would turn, dock nose-to-nose with LM, and pull it free of the used-up rocket. Then it would turn again, and carry LM to moon orbit on its nose.

The little bug-like space ferry, LM, was really two small ships fitted together. The lower half held LM's legs and landing gear. It had a descent (going-down) engine to slow LM's free fall from Apollo to the moon, so that LM would land gently. Once on the moon, the lower half would become a launch pad for its own upper half.

The upper half of LM held the crew cabin. It had an ascent (going-up) engine that would fire to lift the upper half from the moon back to the Apollo orbiting above. The lower half would stay behind. Neither half of LM would ever return to Earth. Once the astronauts were back inside the Apollo command module, the upper half of LM would be left in orbit around the moon or the sun.

Apollo 5, Apollo 9, and Apollo 10 tested LM in flight. Though minor hitches had to be overcome, no sign of trouble with LM threatened Apollo 11's moon landing.

Countdown for Apollo 11

Preparations for the moon flight seemed endless. Together, Apollo 11/Saturn V had more than 10 million parts. So from mid-1968 to the moment of lift-off in 1969, work crews inspected every Apollo and Saturn system and part, even using X rays to look for flaws.

The Apollo 11 astronauts rehearsed the trip. In spacecraft models, they took make-believe flights, with make-believe problems.

Flight scientists checked out all the orbit paths.

Engineers and mathematicians stored facts in computers to help them plot out the flight.

During this complex countdown period, it was Florida's John F. Kennedy Space Center that controlled Apollo 11. After lift-off, control of the flight would pass over to the Manned Spacecraft Center in Houston, Texas.

From there, mission control would be in charge.

Mission Control

Trouble struck Apollo 10 — so fast it took mission control by surprise.

Astronauts Eugene A. Cernan and Thomas P. Stafford in LM (code-named *Snoopy*) had left the command ship (*Charlie Brown*) piloted by John W. Young. Separately the two ships were orbiting the moon.

The LM crew had been checking sites for a future moon landing, and now Cernan and Stafford were ready for a special test: LM's lower half would separate from the upper half. The lower half would move down to the moon's surface. The upper half, with the men, would return to the command ship. During this "separation test," each half of LM would try out its own rocket engine.

At the time, LM was 8.4 miles above the moon. "*Snoopy*

was flying along as solid as a rock," were Stafford's words, and Stafford and Cernan were ready to separate LM's two halves. But suddenly, just before the lower half was cut loose, LM "just took off." It turned sharply in an unexpected direction.

"What was that?" Stafford asked. He steadied the ship with his hand controls, then quickly released LM's lower half and started it down toward the moon.

At that moment, an automatic system was supposed to take over and keep the upper half steady. Instead, LM's upper half again tumbled around wildly. It began to "shiver and shake." It bucked and heaved, up and down, up and down, like a maddened bull.

Mission control heard Cernan's voice clearly but in terror: "Something is wrong. . . . Something went wild. . . . Wait a minute. . . . Got to get this thing. . . . The thing just took off on us. . . ."

For a frightening moment, the astronauts and mission control had one thought: How bad was LM's trouble?

Cernan's heart rate jumped from a normal 60 beats a minute to 128. Stafford, also nervous, grabbed LM's hand controls for the second time and nearly "twisted the control handle off" trying to stop the wild ride.

Stafford and Cernan fired small rockets to slow LM down, and within eight seconds they had brought the ship under control. The emergency was "all over, just like that," and LM headed back to the command ship.

"I don't know what that was, but that was something," radioed Cernan, now calm again. "I thought we were wobbling all over the skies."

As things turned out, Apollo 10's LM trouble was not serious. An automatic control system had failed to take over. So LM's upper half surprised everyone by "galloping off." But Stafford and Cernan, well trained and ready for emergencies, were able to steady the ship.

Suppose they had not been able to manage LM?

Mission control would have stepped in with a substitute flight plan, worked out in advance and carried out automatically by computers. The real danger was slight.

A World-wide Tracking Network

Mission control at Houston, Texas, is one NASA link to a vast tracking network that circles Earth and can reach out to the moon and beyond.

The stations in this network track the flights of all spacecraft, manned and unmanned, using radar, radio

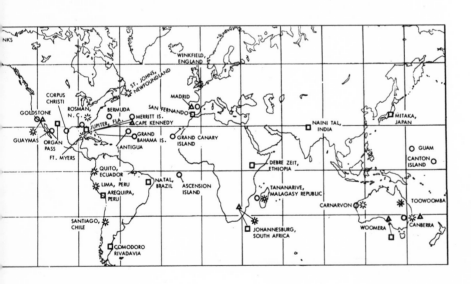

48

○   **Manned space flight network**

✢✢   **Satellite tracking network**

△   **Deep space tracking network**

▢   **Optical tracking network**

"The Big Dish": This 210-foot space antenna at Goldstone, California, can track spacecraft as far as 200 million miles from Earth.

telescopes, telescopic cameras, and radio signals. Each station sends out coded signals which spacecraft automatically relay back. Since radio waves travel at 186,000 miles a second, ground crews can compute the craft's position by the time the signal took to reach it and get back to Earth. Even when a spaceship is at the moon, a signal reaches it and returns to Earth in seconds.

To receive signals returning from great distances, stations use special bowl-shaped antennas. The biggest are three giant antennas at stations almost equally spaced around the world — in California, Spain, and Australia.

49

As Earth turns, first one giant antenna and then the next gathers in the signals. In this way, the signals are never lost (except when a spaceship goes behind the moon or plunges through Earth's atmosphere before splashdown). Often two stations are in range of the ship and can track it at the same time.

The tracking stations check for signs of trouble on a spacecraft; and they calculate its range, speed, altitude, and direction as measured from Earth's center (because the stations are at different altitudes above sea level).

Part of NASA's tracking network keeps tabs on unmanned satellites in deep space.

Another part tracks unmanned craft in near space.

Still another tracks and communicates with manned spacecraft. Apollo 11 was to be tracked by 15 land stations, five ships, eight planes and helicopters, and cable, telephone, teletype, TV, and radio circuits.

The Manned Spacecraft Center

Mission control is just one corner of the 1,620 acre Manned Spacecraft Center in Houston, Texas. The Center looks like the campus of a big college, with its graveled paths, clipped lawns, parking lots, evergreen shrubs, shady oak and pine trees, and low buildings.

About 90 buildings make up the Center. By 1969, just before Apollo 11, more than 13,000 people worked there. They, too, gave it the air of a college. There were professors, scientists, engineers, computer experts, mathematicians, research workers, secretaries, and even "students" — the always-studying astronauts themselves.

Mission control is the best-known part of the Manned Spacecraft Center. Taking in information from the tracking stations around the world, it guides and directs all U.S. manned space flights.

The mission control staff — on day and night shifts during a space mission — work in a huge, chunky building with no windows. This is protection against the chance that a storm or hurricane could smash windows and wreck TV sets, computers, and other instruments. If this happened while men were in space or on the moon, the astronauts could get back to Earth without mission control's help — but the trip would be very risky.

Flight controllers are the people who direct manned missions. They work in a large room with rows of small computer units, or consoles. They are in constant touch with the spaceship, relaying information to the crew, and seeing that the ship stays on course, reaches its destination, and brings the crew home safely.

Flashing lights on the console show the flight controller what problem the computer is working on. Numbers in a code flash constantly across small TV screens telling the condition of an engine, for instance, or how much fuel is being used. On the walls, huge maps light up to show the ship's course.

Studying constantly the console lights, the TV screens, and the maps, flight controllers detect instantly if the ship is straying off course. At once, computers are put to work. They make quick calculations and relay orders — needed instantly — to correct the flight path.

Computers and Spaceships

The computers at mission control are electronically linked to small computers riding in the spaceship. Thus, changes ordered in Houston are made automatically aboard ship. But how does a computer work?

A computer is a "brain machine," but no computer thinks on its own. It only uses information men feed into it. It never thinks up a single new idea.

A computer works automatically. It stores information fed into it and sorts it out. It may apply the information to a problem and come up with an answer. But the decision of whether or not to use the computer's automatic answer is made by a man, who *thinks*.

A computer needs a program. Before a flight, engineers feed a flight program into the computer in a special code language of electronic signals. The program includes information and instructions to guide a normal flight — and also to cover emergencies that might come up.

During the flight, new information on the ship's progress is fed in. If a course correction is needed, the computer will make it automatically, based on the preplanned program and the new information coming in.

A computer is lightning fast. A computer does no work a man could not do — if he had time. The information in the computer is put there by men. The decision about using the computer's answers is up to men. Then why do men need computers at all?

A computer works millions of times as fast as a man's brain. Computer speed is measured in *nanoseconds*. A nanosecond is one thousandth of a millionth of a second. In one full second, a modern computer could make 15

million additions — a lifetime of brain work for a man with pad and pencil.

Without computers, man could not go into space.

Spaceships travel at speeds up to 25,000 miles an hour, or seven miles a second. At such speeds, no crew could think and react fast enough to plot a course and make the thousands of tiny course corrections.

Imagine that a manned spaceship is returning to Earth.

Mission control, Houston: Flight controllers follow a moon landing on rows of computer consoles, huge wall maps, and TV screens.

When should the braking rockets be fired? At mission control, computers figure the answer instantly. The braking rockets go off at just the right moment and in just the right place. The ship slows and curves for its splashdown.

A recovery ship is standing by. Exactly where, they want to know, will the astronauts come down? The needed information is coming into mission control from the tracking stations. Computers take in the information and pinpoint the splashdown. The location is flashed on TV screens at mission control and relayed to the recovery ship at the same time. Before the astronauts drop into the water, the recovery ship may already be speeding in to pick them up.

Computers are reliable and fast. They can do a tremendous amount of work without breaking down. They give flight controllers the most important gift of all: time.

Training the Astronauts

In 1959, after tests and interviews, the famous seven original Mercury astronauts were picked from more than 500 applicants. By 1969 the U.S. had 52 astronauts.

Since only three men at a time could make an Apollo flight, people sometimes wondered what kept the astronauts busy. Most of the time, they were putting in long hours of study.

At the Manned Spacecraft Center in Houston, the astronauts' home base, the men worked in laboratories, classrooms, and special-equipment-testing areas. They flew to other parts of the country to check out new equipment, study astronomy, learn about spaceships and rocketry, and go through moon-landing techniques. They even went through jungle-survival training. To train a man for possible moon flight, at least three years were needed.

Each Apollo flight involved nine astronauts. Three were in the regular crew. Three were in the back-up crew, ready to take over if anything happened to the regular crew. And three were in the support crew which helped test the other two crews and kept in touch with them from flight control during practice moon flights.

Apollo crews had to know how to deal with every emergency anyone could imagine coming up. During practice flights, flight controllers would throw the practice spacecraft into emergency situations without warning, and future moon pilots had to be able to deal with them. Day after day, the astronauts practiced on the ground what they hoped they would *never* have to do in space.

When a crew returned from space, they spent weeks at the Center teaching other astronauts what they had learned and reviewing each problem in their own flight.

And so the Apollo 7 crew helped the crew of Apollo 8. Apollo 8 passed along advice to Apollo 9. Apollo 9 did the same for Apollo 10. And from Apollo 10 the crew of Apollo 11 learned much about piloting their own moon-ship.

All through the early summer of 1969, the men of Apollo 11 rehearsed their moon-landing flight. By mid-July, they were ready.

Lift-off for Apollo 11 was at hand.

Off to the Moon

A STEADY STREAM of people, young and old, began moving toward the Kennedy Space Center in Florida. By mid-July it had attracted a million visitors. They came from all parts of the country. They came alone, they came in groups, they came with families. They hiked, they biked, they flew. Cars, trailers, buses, and motorcycles jammed roads and highways. Motels and hotels were filled.

People came with cameras, binoculars, tape recorders, sketchpads. They came for many reasons, but mainly they came to be a part of history. They wanted to watch the Apollo 11 lift-off with their own eyes. They wanted to be able to say they had seen the first moment of the great moon-landing flight, on July 16, 1969.

It was the start of a new age for man. No one would

Apollo 11/Saturn V poised on the launch pad. A double exposure shows its target, the moon, rising behind it.

forget 1969, just as no one has forgotten 1492.

As a safety measure, visitors could not get too close to the Saturn V rocket. But there it stood, upright, some three miles away, gleaming white in the sunlight — and whiter still under floodlights at night.

The night before lift-off, the three Apollo 11 astronauts went to bed early. They were Neil A. Armstrong, the commander; Edwin E. (Buzz) Aldrin, Jr., the LM pilot; and Michael Collins, the command ship pilot. The men had much in common. Each had been born in 1930. Each was an experienced jet pilot. And each had been on space missions before.

Armstrong, calm and quick-thinking, had been the commander of Gemini 8. He had performed the first space docking in history, joining Gemini with an unmanned Agena target ship. Later, when Gemini 8 tumbled out of control, he brought it down safely in a wild emergency splashdown in the Pacific Ocean.

Aldrin, a brilliant space scientist, had served as co-pilot of Gemini 12 and had made a five-and-a-half-hour spacewalk, evaluating new equipment and space tools.

Collins, an all-round astronaut, had been the co-pilot of Gemini 10. He had walked in space twice and had performed a difficult double-docking task, linking up twice with Agena target ships.

Armstrong would be the first man to walk on the moon, and Aldrin would be the second. Collins, orbiting overhead in the command ship, would not touch down on the moon. But he was pleased to be part of the crew. "I'm going 99.99 per cent of the way," he explained.

58

On the morning of July 16, the men got up at about 4:15 a.m. They had a healthy breakfast of orange juice, steak, scrambled eggs, toast, coffee. Soon they were in white spacesuits and on the way to Pad 39A. An elevator lifted them to the top of the Saturn V.

Armstrong boarded and sat on the left side. Then came

59

The Apollo 11 astronauts: left to right, Neil A. Armstrong, Michael Collins, and Edwin E. Aldrin, Jr.

Collins on the right, with Aldrin in the center of the command ship, code-named *Columbia*. LM, code-named *Eagle*, was stored, with legs folded, between the service module and the front of the third-stage rocket.

At Pad 39A a million faces were turned to the rocket. Millions upon millions more watched on TV beamed around the world. What they could not see were Armstrong, Aldrin, and Collins inside Apollo 11, running through testing patterns and checking out systems and switch settings on the control panel. All was in perfect order.

"Lift-off . . . we have a lift-off. . . ."

The countdown minutes dwindled into the final seconds.

"Twenty seconds and counting," called flight control. ". . . 12 . . . 11 . . . 10 . . . 9 . . . ignition sequence starts . . . 6 . . . 5 . . . 4 . . . 3 . . . 2 . . . 1 . . . zero . . . all engines running." As the countdown ended, powerful jets of steam spurted from the pad below the rocket. Blinding orange flame leaped out, slamming into the ground. Intense, glaring light dazzled onlookers. Black clouds of smoke billowed up and spread far. Then the flame turned white and formed into a thick column that seemed to push the rocket up through its own fiery cloud into the clouds above.

The battle against Earth's gravity was on. Slowly, silently, the rocket rose straight up like a giant elevator. Then came a deafening, shattering, roar of explosions. The ground shook, and for miles around everyone felt the thunderous power of Saturn V as its 7,500,000 pounds of thrust lifted 6,500,000 pounds of weight.

"Lift-off . . . we have a lift-off 32 minutes past the hour," came the call from flight control.

Apollo was on target for the moon. At lift-off, the moon was exactly 218,096 miles away.

"Go, go, go," shouted many people at the scene. "Go, baby, go." Thousands more clapped with pleasure and with pride. Others stood in silent prayer, in tears of joy, or in hushed awe.

"Lift-off on Apollo 11," continued flight control. "Tower cleared." Instantly, ground command of the flight switched from Florida to mission control in Houston, Texas.

The ground no longer shook. The air was still again. All was silent. An orange-black cloud of smoke hugged the ground and drifted out to sea. Majestically, Saturn V soared straight upward, curved out over the Atlantic Ocean, and climbed into position for a trip around Earth.

In two-and-a-half minutes, Saturn V was out of sight, swallowed up by a blue sky. The second-stage rocket fired. Ten minutes later, the third-stage rocket fired and put Apollo 11 into Earth orbit, at a speed of 17,500 miles an hour, 118 miles above the surface.

The men were now weightless. While circling Earth, they again checked out systems and switches and replotted their moon course. Then, two-and-a-half hours after lift-off, the third-stage rocket fired again, for nearly six minutes. This raised Apollo 11's speed to 24,250 miles an hour and drove it out of Earth orbit.

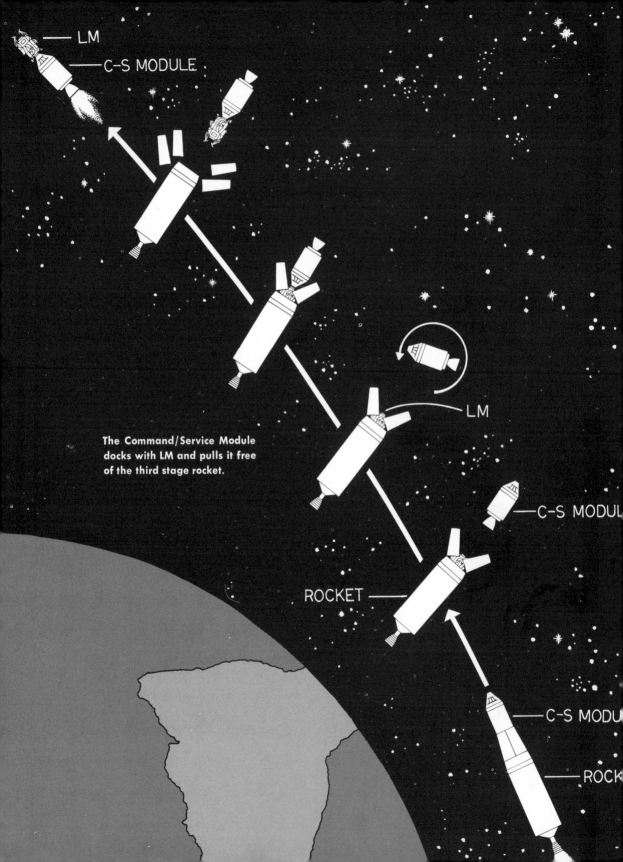

LM

C-S MODULE

LM

The Command/Service Module
docks with LM and pulls it free
of the third stage rocket.

C-S MODUL

ROCKET

C-S MODU

ROCK

"You are well on your way now," mission control radioed. Apollo 11 was off to the moon.

"We have a happy home."

The important and tricky maneuver of docking with LM was at hand. The command ship, *Columbia*, had to pull the LM, *Eagle*, out of the front end of the third-stage booster. As command ship pilot, Collins was in charge.

First Collins separated *Columbia* (and its service module) from *Eagle* and the booster rocket. *Eagle* was now visible at the front end of the spent rocket. Collins flew *Columbia* off to one side and turned the ship so that it faced *Eagle*. Then he flew back to it.

Gently and easily, Collins linked *Columbia* nose-to-nose with *Eagle*. The used-up rocket booster was released and sent into orbit around the sun. *Columbia* and *Eagle*, flying together, turned again and headed toward the moon. The next time they separated would be during moon orbit.

After the docking, the crew settled down to the routine duties of the eight-day mission. They checked equipment, studied their flight plan, made navigational readings. Like fussy housewives, they tidied their moonship. And they prepared TV shows for Earthlings.

"We have a happy home," Collins said during a telecast. "There's plenty of room for the three of us, and I think we're all learning to find our favorite little corner to sit in." Weightlessness, he went on, was comfortable. "But after a while," he said, "you sort of get tired of rattling around and banging off the ceiling and the floor

and the sides, so you tend to find a little corner some-
where and put your knees up . . . to wedge yourself in
and that seems more at home."

The food was good, too. Collins radioed back, "My
compliments to the chef. The salmon salad is outstand-
ing." Other food, mostly in plastic bags, included bacon
squares, shrimp cocktail, spaghetti and meat sauce,
chicken and rice, chicken stew, pork and potatoes,
brownies, butterscotch pudding, coffee. The men
squirted water into the bags with a water-pistol to "mush
up" their food. But they also had fresh apples and
oranges.

On July 17, the second day, mission control ordered
Apollo 11 to fire its rockets for three seconds, making a
mid-course correction.

Apollo 11 was moving in two ways. It was going
forward, its speed decreasing as it moved away from
Earth; and it was rotating three turns an hour so that the
sun would heat it evenly. If the ship did not make these
"barbecuing" turns, the side in darkness would freeze at
250 degrees below zero Fahrenheit. The sunlit side
would bake at 250 degrees above zero Fahrenheit.

When Apollo 11 was 133,400 miles away, Armstrong
asked mission control if rain was falling in Houston.
"Looks like you have a circulation of clouds in the area,"
said Armstrong. "Did that have any rain in it this morning?" Houston answered: "Our report from outside says
it's raining." "It looks like it ought to be clearing up
pretty soon," said Armstrong. "The western edge of the
cloud pattern has almost reached you." Armstrong was
right. It did stop raining in Houston.

By July 18, the third day, Apollo 11 was three quarters of the way to the moon. Armstrong and Aldrin showed Earthlings the inside of *Eagle*, the moon-lander, by way of TV. As the hatch leading into *Eagle* opened, Collins said, "It's just like a refrigerator when you open the door. The light goes on." They reported that *Eagle* was in perfect working order.

"It was like perfect."

On July 19, the ship slowed down to 1,700 miles an hour, its slowest speed. Then Apollo 11 came under the control of the moon's gravity, and it picked up speed again. Soon it was ready to make its first swing around the moon.

Once behind the moon, the men had to fire the main rocket to slow down Apollo 11. It would have to fire just right to allow Apollo to be captured by the moon's gravity. When the ship came out from behind the moon, Armstrong radioed back: "It was like perfect."

The pull of the moon's gravity now gripped Apollo 11 in orbit, its speed dipping to around 3,700 miles an hour. Each full orbit of the moon took two hours.

As they orbited, the men sent more TV pictures back to Earth. Then they began to prepare for the big day ahead — July 20 — and the landing on the moon.

During the ship's 11th orbit, Armstrong and Aldrin put on their spacesuits and crawled into *Eagle* through a small tunnel for a final check of equipment.

On the 13th orbit, with both men aboard, *Eagle* would leave *Columbia* and start down to the moon.

First Men on the Moon

JUST BEFORE THE 13th orbit of the moon, mission control radioed: "Apollo 11, Houston. We're go for undocking." This was the signal to separate *Eagle* from *Columbia*.

Apollo 11 disappeared behind the moon and the world waited for word that both ships were flying alone. About 45 minutes later they came around again — separately.

"How does it look?" mission control asked.

"The *Eagle* has wings," answered Armstrong. Then he added, "Looking good."

For 15 minutes, the two ships flew only a few feet apart. During this time, Armstrong and Aldrin checked the *Eagle* inside while Collins, from *Columbia's* window, looked over its outside, especially the landing gear. Then *Columbia* fired small rockets and moved into a new orbit, about two miles from *Eagle*.

66

"I think you've got a fine-looking flying machine there, *Eagle*, despite the fact that you're upside down," Collins radioed jokingly.

"*Somebody's* upside down," Armstrong replied.

No one could say who *was* upside down. In space, without gravity or landmarks, there is no "up" or "down."

"Going right down U.S. 1, Mike," said Armstrong, to show that *Eagle* had clear sailing ahead.

Now both *Columbia* and *Eagle* went behind the moon again. On the far side, *Eagle* was to fire the rocket engine to start it down toward the surface.

"Mike, how did it go?" mission control asked when *Columbia* reappeared on the near side.

"Listen, babe, everything's going just swimmingly. Beautiful," came the answer from Collins. The LM lander had successfully fired its rocket engine.

"Great. We're standing by for *Eagle*."

"O.K., he's coming around," said Collins.

Two minutes later, *Eagle* radioed Houston that all was well, and continued its drop into the unknown.

Now, every foot of the way was a new adventure for man. Apollo 10's LM, *Snoopy*, had come to about 45,000 feet from the surface. But now, *Eagle* was below that point. Never before had man come so close to the moon.

Inside the ship, the number 99 flashed on a computer — a code signal that Armstrong had a few seconds to make a decision: to refire the engine and drop to the surface . . . or to stay in moon orbit, link up with *Columbia*, and go home.

Armstrong pushed a "proceed" button. The engine

restarted. Down flew *Eagle*, its rocket engine acting as a brake. As it slowed, it began to "fall" out of orbit — 40,000 feet . . . 20,000 feet . . . 15,000 feet . . . 5,000 feet. Houston radioed, "You are go for landing."

"Tranquility Base here."

Moving forward tail first, *Eagle's* windows were still tilted upward, away from the surface. Armstrong at the controls and Aldrin next to him — calling out the ship's forward speed and rate of drop — were flying blind. They were relying on computers and flight instruments.

A smooth target landing area seven miles long and three miles wide had been charted out before the flight. But now, below the ship and not too far ahead of it — unseen by Armstrong and Aldin — appeared a crater filled with rocks and boulders. *Eagle's* computer had guided the ship to the crater instead of to the target area — now four miles behind them.

Actually, the computer was working perfectly well. Why, then, was it moving the ship toward a crater instead of toward the landing target?

When *Eagle* separated from *Columbia*, two small rockets were turned off to keep their flames from damaging a radio antenna. This had caused a slight change in *Eagle's* speed and flight path. From this *changed* position, and later changes too small to notice at the time, the computer was guiding *Eagle* to a landing target — but the wrong one!

Now, as *Eagle* arched toward the surface, it turned its legs downward into touchdown position. For the first time, the men could see the surface from *Eagle's* win-

dows. Instead of the smooth landing area he expected, Armstrong saw the rock-filled crater passing below.

What, he wondered, was wrong? Armstrong had to make a fast decision whether to let the computer guide *Eagle* in for a landing, or whether to work the controls manually. He decided to let the computer guide *Eagle* for a few moments — then to take over himself.

The Apollo planners had foreseen such a situation. A few weeks before the flight, Armstrong had explained, "As we come down lower, we'll be able to evaluate the landing site better. If required, we will alter that landing point. . . . As we come through the 500-foot level or thereabouts, we'll probably take control manually and fly to the precise touchdown point."

69

With windows (on either side of the ladder) turned skyward, Armstrong and Aldrin could not see the crater passing below until LM's legs turned downward into touchdown position.

Now, Armstrong prepared to do just that. With his right hand, he worked the attitude control, which took care of *Eagle's* position and direction as it dropped. With his left hand, he worked a switch that regulated the rate of drop. Meanwhile, he kept watching both the fuel gauge and the boulder-filled crater below.

Armstrong had taken over from the computer and was flying *Eagle* in alone. There was nothing to rely on now but years of training and tremendous skill as a pilot.

At mission control, warning lights had begun flashing on control panels — signals of an overloaded and over-worked computer "calling out alarms." At first, no one was certain why the warning lights were flashing. Was *Eagle* in unexpected danger? Mission control thought not. It told *Eagle* to continue its drop.

At that point, the ship was supposed to be dropping *down* faster than it was moving forward. Instead, it was suddenly moving *forward* fast, and barely dropping. *Eagle* was dropping only one foot a second, but was skimming right above the surface at 47 feet a second. And as it swept over the crater, there was little fuel left.

Aldrin called in the position: ". . . 300 feet, down 3½, 47 forward . . . down one a minute. 1½ down. 70. Got the shadow out there. 50, down at 2½. 19 forward . . . 3½ down. 220 feet. 13 forward . . . coming down nicely . . . 75 feet . . . things looking good. Down a half. 6 forward."

Mission control reported back: "*Sixty seconds.*"

Computer warnings kept flashing. *Eagle's* fuel supply kept dropping. Mission control radioed: "Go for landing."

Eagle answered: "Lights on. Down 2½. Forward, forward. Good. 40 feet, down 2½. Picking up some dust. 30

70

Computers guided Apollo 11's LM toward this crater, photographed by the crew. In the crater's rocky bottom, LM might have landed at a tilt great enough to make lift-off and return to Earth impossible.

feet, 2½ down. Faint shadow. 4 forward. 4 forward. Drifting to the right a little . . . down a half.

"Thirty seconds," called mission control.

Skillfully working the hand controls, Armstrong had steered *Eagle* past the crater. The ship blew out a swirling cloud of dust as it inched down to the surface.

Aldrin said, "Forward. Drifting right. . : ."

Long metal probes on *Eagle's* legs touched the surface. As they did, a blue light flashed in the cockpit. "Contact light," called in *Eagle*. "O.K. engine stop. Engine arm off. 413 is in."

"We copy you down, *Eagle*," said mission control.

"Tranquility Base here," answered Armstrong. "The *Eagle* has landed."

The ship was down, 20,000 feet beyond the original target zone. It had "landed long" — but it had landed safely on a flat plain in the Sea of Tranquility, about 1,200 feet from the rocky crater. And it had come to within 30 or 40 seconds of running out of fuel.

"Roger, Tranquility," mission control said. "We copy you on the ground. You've got a bunch of guys about to turn blue. We're breathing again. Thanks a lot."

It was 4:17 p.m., Eastern Daylight Time. The moon, which never had known man or his time, now had both.

Armstrong had shown that man is needed in space flight. A computer can't do everything. Certainly, it can't work out answers to *unforeseen* emergencies.

"Be advised there are lots of smiling faces in this room," said mission control, after *Eagle* landed.

"There are two of them up here," said the *Eagle* crew.

"And don't forget one in the command module," said
Collins, who had been almost forgotten as he circled in
Columbia, 70 miles above the moon.

"We came in peace for all mankind."

Now Aldrin and Armstrong had time to rest. Several
hours later, they struggled into their spacesuits, boots,
helmets, gloves. They also put on their "portable life-
support systems," back packs that carried oxygen for
breathing, a water cooling system, and communications.
Then they depressurized the LM cabin. When the pre-
sure was down to zero, Armstrong opened the hatch,
turned around, and backed out onto the porch, a small
platform above the ship's nine-step ladder.

"O.K., Houston, I'm on the porch," he reported. On the
second step Armstrong pulled a rope to release a section
on the side of *Eagle*. A TV camera automatically began
to take pictures. And for the first time, Earthlings clustered around their TV sets could see, as well as hear, the
man on the moon.

"We can see you coming down the ladder now," said
Houston.

Armstrong answered, "I'm at the foot of the ladder.
The LM footpads are only depressed in the surface about
one or two inches, although the surface appears to be
very, very fine-grained as you get close to it. It's almost
like a powder. It's very fine. I'm going to step off the LM
now."

Seconds later his booted left foot pressed down on the
moon's surface.

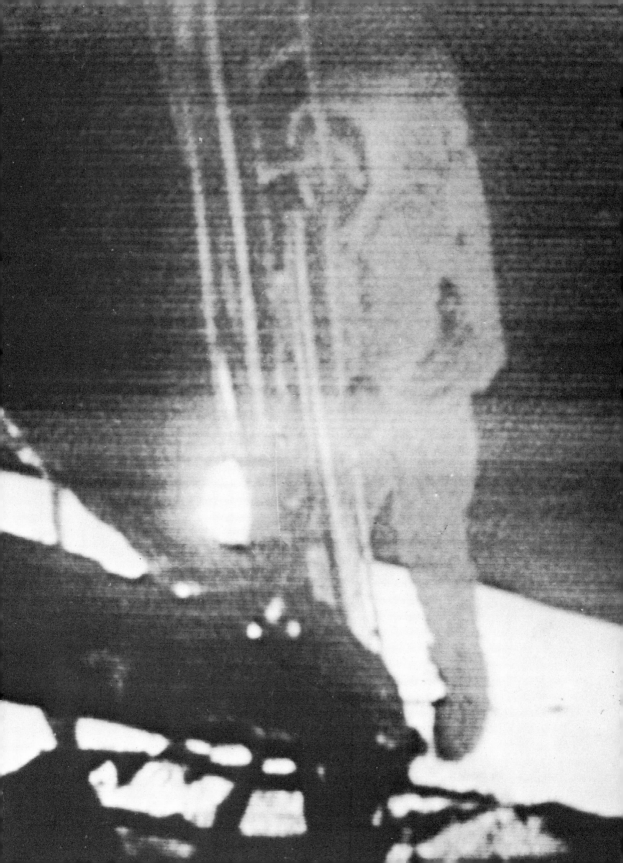

"That's one small step for a man, one giant leap for mankind," said Armstrong.

He stared out on a bleak, desert-like scene. The moon had a dull grayish and dirty brown look except where bright glaring sunlight blinded the eye, or where deep black shadows darkened the surface. The surface was lumpy, rocky, pitted, cratered. It had a powdery and sandy feel and in some places was even slippery.

"The surface is fine and powdery," Armstrong said. "I can pick it up loosely with my toe. It does adhere in fine layers like powdered charcoal to the sole and the sides of my boots. I only go in a small fraction of an inch, maybe an eighth of an inch, but I can see the footprints of my boots and the treads in the fine sandy particles. There seems to be no difficulty in moving around . . . actually no trouble to walk around."

At first he took short steps like a man testing the sea at a strange beach, feeling his way over the surface. It held his weight easily enough. He did not sink in deep. He noticed that even *Eagle's* heavy footpads hardly sank into the soil. Nor did he have trouble keeping his balance in the moon's one-sixth-of-Earth's gravity. He weighed 60 pounds — with spacesuit, back pack, and all. On Earth he'd have weighed 360 pounds.

The soil, loose and powdery on top, was firm and solid underneath. Armstrong collected soil and rock samples and took pictures. He also changed the position of the TV camera to show more of the moon.

"The moon has a stark beauty of its own," reported Armstrong. "It's like much of the high desert of the United States."

75

Earthlings who watched Neil Armstrong step onto the moon could barely make out what was happening. The fuzzy TV image made the event look like a scene from an old-time science fiction movie.

Nearly 20 minutes passed. Now it was Aldrin's chance.

"Ready for me to come out?" Aldrin asked Armstrong.

Armstrong said, "O.K." — then reminded Aldrin to adjust some of his equipment. Aldrin started out.

"You're right at the edge of the porch," Armstrong said, as Aldrin moved out farther. Aldrin stopped. "Now I want to back up and partially close the hatch — making sure not to lock it on the way out."

"A particularly good thought," quipped Armstrong.

"That's our home for the next couple of hours and I want to take care of it," Aldrin went on. "O.K. . . . I'm on the top step. It's a very simple matter to hop down from one step to the next."

Aldrin came down the ladder. From the first step he enjoyed himself, for he leaped back up three feet to the bottom rung of the ladder. Twice more he did this, to show how simple it was to jump on the moon. He looked around to admire the view.

"Beautiful, beautiful," he said.

"Isn't that something?" agreed Armstrong. "Magnificent sight down here."

"Magnificent desolation," added Aldrin. He told of seeing thousands of small craters and sharp rocks of many shapes and materials. Later, he ran a short way — a "first." Armstrong had been the first man to walk on the moon, but Aldrin was the first to run there. Walking, Aldrin took long strides, putting one foot down directly in front of the other. Then he tried a "kangaroo hop" — jumping with both feet at the same time.

"Isn't it fun?" said Armstrong.

76

Soon after, Armstrong fastened a stainless steel plaque to *Eagle's* front landing gear. The plaque showed Earth's Western and Eastern Hemispheres. Armstrong read the words on the plaque:

Both men then planted an American flag. The flag seemed to fly unfurled. Thin wire and springs held it in such a way that it appeared to ripple. But it was motionless on the plain, where no air stirred.

Science on the Moon

ARMSTRONG AND ALDRIN had simple but important scientific tasks to do. Before they went on with them, mission control asked both men to move inside the range of the TV camera.

"The President of the United States would like to say a few words to you," explained Houston.

President Nixon had put through a radio-telephone call from the White House to Tranquility Base. The astronauts stood at attention together near the American flag. Then the President said:

"Hello, Neil and Buzz. . . . This certainly has to be the most historic phone call ever made.

"I just can't tell you how proud we all are of what you have done. . . . Because of what you have done, the heavens have become part of man's world. . . . All the people on this Earth are truly one . . . one in their pride of what you have done . . . and one in our prayers that you will return safely to Earth."

Man's first hour on the moon soon drew to a close, and still there was much work ahead for science. Armstrong and Aldrin would perform tasks on the moon's surface for all the scientists back on Earth who could not be there themselves.

Using Science Skills

Armstrong had already used one key scientific skill: observing. In the first moments of his moon walk, he had observed the soil and described it as fine, powdery, and sandy. A few minutes later, he had radioed: "This is very interesting. It's a very soft surface, but here and there . . . I run into a very hard surface, but it appears to be cohesive [stuck-together] material of the same sort."

Observing carefully is just one scientific skill. Others include: measuring, experimenting, recording information, collecting samples, and classifying (putting things in groups according to likenesses and differences).

The skills of science help men to find new links between old facts. Scientists ask questions. To find the answers they plan and carry out experiments and record the results. Then they think over these results and draw their conclusions. And every answer they find leads to new questions, new experiments, new conclusions. In this way, science advances man to new frontiers of knowledge. As one scientist puts it, "Science is the effort of the human mind to enlighten itself by evidence."

On the moon's surface, Armstrong and Aldrin both worked skillfully in the ways of science.

As soon as he stepped down from *Eagle*, Armstrong had scooped up rocks and soil with a special tool, a bag on the end of a 25-inch handle. Quickly, he stuffed this first small moon sampling into a leg pocket on his space-suit. Now, if an emergency forced *Eagle* to leave the moon suddenly, some of its surface would go along for study by Earth scientists.

Armstrong then collected many more rocks with a box-like scoop and long metal tongs. He put the rocks and soil in plastic bags, then sealed the bags inside two air-tight aluminum boxes. With a rope-and-pulley system, much like a clothesline, he hoisted the boxes aboard *Eagle*. When *Eagle* returned, scientists would have a treasure of materials to study and to classify — in all, about 50 pounds of moon rock and soil.

Time was flying, but the moon explorers set up three scientific instruments.

Trapping the Solar Wind

Soon after Aldrin stepped out on the surface, mission control announced, "Buzz is erecting the solar wind experiment."

This was the first of the three experiments, a sheet of aluminum foil, about four feet long and one foot wide. The foil, mounted on a telescoped pole, unrolled much like a window shade. After opening out the foil, Aldrin faced it toward the sun.

The foil's job was to capture tiny particles that move

Edwin Aldrin unfurls the solar wind experiment. With no atmosphere to spread light, the contrast between light and shadow is very sharp.

out steadily from the sun at supersonic speed. Scientists call this flow of particles the "solar wind."

If the experiment worked, the foil would collect particles of such thin, rare gases as helium, argon, neon, xenon, krypton. The particles would stick to the foil much as sand sticks to a freshly-painted surface. Before the astronauts left, they would roll up the aluminum foil, store it in a vacuum box, and bring it aboard *Eagle*.

In its first hour, the aluminum foil captured trillions of particles. By studying such particles captured on the moon, scientists hoped to know more about the sun.

A Moonquake Meter

The second experiment Aldrin set up was a seismometer, or "moonquake meter." For a year or more, it would detect moonquakes, volcanic action, landslides, rock slides, meteor bombardments, or other disturbances or vibrations.

Aldrin carried this miniature science station to a level spot, fixed it in place on the surface, and reported, "I have the seismic experiment flipped over now."

Immediately, it began to send information back to Earth. The seismometer quickly recorded a possible moonquake and tremors from landslides in craters close by. It even recorded the astronauts' footsteps as they walked away.

The seismometer would give scientists fresh clues to the moon's composition. It might help them settle one of the biggest debates among scientists: whether the moon, at present, is "hot and alive" or "cold and dead." Throughout the two-week-long day, when sunlight powered

the seismometer's solar cells, it would "listen" for activity in the moon's crust.

The Laser Reflector

Next Aldrin set up a two-foot-square reflector, a series of 100 mirrors. In this experiment, scientists and mapmakers would aim and "fire" lasers at the reflector-target. A laser is a thin beam of highly-concentrated and intensely-focused light. Each laser would bounce from the reflector right back to where it came from on Earth. Since scientists know that light travels at 186,000 miles a

With LM in the background, Edwin Aldrin walks near the science experiments. His footprints (in the foreground) will probably last a million years, since there is no weather erosion on the moon.

second, they could figure out Earth-moon distances by timing a laser's round trip.

Information from the laser experiment may some day settle another argument among scientists: *Are Earth and the moon drifting apart?* Some believe they are, but not by much, perhaps an inch a year.

If the returning laser strikes slightly off the point it was sent from, scientists might also learn if the continents on Earth are slowly drifting apart. Still another problem the laser experiment may help solve is how much the moon "wobbles" as it spins.

"The laser reflector has been installed," Aldrin reported. Little time remained for moon exploring, and the scientific work would have to be speeded up.

Two Core Tubes

Mission control reported: "Neil Armstrong has been on the surface now about an hour and 50 minutes. . . . Buzz Aldrin is collecting a core tube sample."

Aldrin was driving a long tube into the stubborn surface with a hammer.

"I hope you're watching how hard I have to hit this into the ground to the tune of about five inches," Aldrin said, slamming the tube with all his strength. "It almost looks wet." This was the first of two samples Aldrin would get by driving a tube into the surface, then pulling it up with its core packed full of rock and soil. The second core was even harder to get. "The second one took two hands on the hammer and I was putting pretty good dents in the top of the rod," said Aldrin. The two core samples from *below* the surface would show scientists the beginnings of the moon's rock layer formations.

Time on the moon was beginning to run out when mission control radioed this reminder to Armstrong: "We would like you to get two core tubes and the solar wind experiment. Two core tubes and the solar wind."

The laser reflector and the seismometer would remain on the moon.

"We're running a little low on time," called mission control. "Head on up the ladder, Buzz."

Aldrin walked back to *Eagle* and climbed aboard. A few minutes later, Armstrong followed, bringing with him the solar wind foil and the core tubes. Now the men began to prepare for lift-off.

"O.K., the hatch is closed and latched," said Aldrin, "and we're up by it secure."

Soon *Eagle* would be repressurized — ready to leave the moon.

"Everything went beautifully."

Eagle and the astronauts had been on the moon for nearly 22 hours. Armstrong had walked on the surface for a little more than two hours, Aldrin for a little less than two hours. They had planted the American flag, put up a plaque of peace, set up two experiments, brought back a third, collected soil and rock, and pulled out core samples. They had left behind medals and shoulder patches in memory of two dead Russian cosmonauts — Yuri Gagarin and Vladimir Komarov — and three dead American astronauts — Virgil Grissom, Roger Chaffee, and Edward White.

All during this time, Michael Collins, alone, had circled the moon 17 times, 70 miles overhead, patiently waiting to link *Columbia* with *Eagle* again. And for 45 minutes each time he passed behind the moon, Collins could not make contact with anyone.

Now mission control called Collins to tell him that Armstrong and Aldrin were safe inside their ship.

"Everything went beautifully," said Houston.

"Hallelujah!" answered Collins.

He would not be riding alone in space much longer.

Home Again – Safely

ARMSTRONG AND ALDRIN climbed back into *Eagle*. They threw back onto the moon all that was not needed for the return trip — back packs, boots, and hoses.

After a relaxed meal and a long rest, they prepared to lift off from the moon. Their launch pad was *Eagle's* own lower half. Small exploding charges had unattached the upper and lower halves. The upper half, with its ascent engine, was free to lift off alone.

The engine had worked well in tests on Earth. But now it was on the moon and this was no test. If the engine did not fire, both astronauts would be stranded. They would die in three days for lack of oxygen.

"You are cleared for take-off," radioed Houston.

"We're Number One on the runway," answered Aldrin. He radioed the countdown and the lift-off:

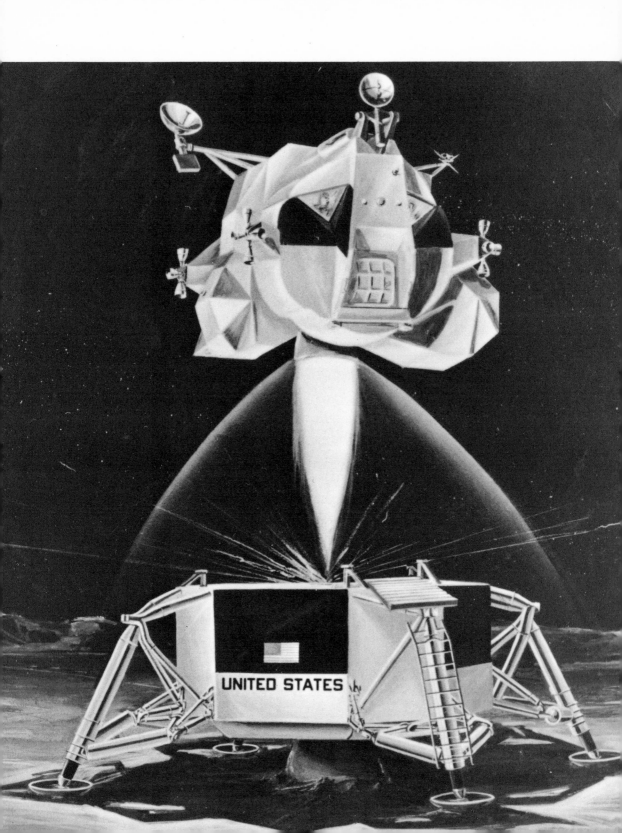

". . . nine, eight, seven, six, five. First stage engine on ascent. Proceed. Beautiful . . . 26 . . . 36 feet per second up . . . very smooth, very quiet ride."

The ship had lifted off in style. It rose swiftly, like a high-speed elevator, for it was much lighter in the moon's weak gravity.

"Right down U.S. 1," radioed *Eagle*.

A few hours later *Eagle* caught up with *Columbia* and got ready to dock. Suddenly, both ships began to rattle around. They had been out of position for the docking and had banged into each other. But in three minutes, all was under control again.

Aldrin and Armstrong squeezed through a tunnel connecting the ships. Collins, who had been alone in moon orbit for nearly 28 hours, was glad to see them. The men sealed the hatch, and separated *Eagle* from the command ship. *Eagle* was too low on fuel to be fired into orbit around the sun and was left in moon orbit.

Soon after, *Columbia* fired its rocket engine, pulled free of the moon's gravity, and started its long, coasting ride back to Earth.

"Time to open up the LRL doors."

"How did it go?" called mission control.

"Time to open up the LRL doors," was the answer. LRL was the Lunar Receiving Laboratory near Houston — a building set aside for examining astronauts and their moon samples after a moon mission. Until 21 days after lift-off from the moon, the Apollo 11 crew would be

A drawing of LM's upper half lifting off, leaving the lower half behind.

in quarantine. The men could not leave the laboratory or come in contact with anyone from the outside.

The idea was to protect Earthlings from any strange and deadly moon germs the men might have brought back. Few — if any — scientists believed the moon had life. Yet no one was certain. And if it existed, moon life could threaten Earth life. This is why:

Moon germs might be different from Earth germs. Human bodies have built up resistance to most Earth germs. But if humans were invaded by hostile moon germs, their bodies would have no way of protecting themselves. Plant life on Earth could also be threatened. Moon germs could mean death to life on Earth.

As a safety measure, men and materials that came back from the moon would be whisked straight to the Lunar Receiving Laboratory for examination and treatment.

"Task accomplished . . . July 1969."

On the return trip, the men beamed lively TV shows back to Earth. Collins, showing how you might drink weightless water, flipped over a spoonful of water and the drops began to float by him. Then he "snapped" at the drops with his mouth to capture and swallow them.

Later, in a more serious mood, Aldrin spoke. "We feel that this flight stands as a symbol of the insatiable curiosity of all mankind to explore the unknown."

On July 24, 1969, *Columbia* began curving down over Australia. The service module was freed 5,300 miles above the surface. The heat shield turned white as *Columbia* ripped into Earth's atmosphere. The ship's speed dropped from 24,700 to about 170 miles an hour.

Two big parachutes opened to slow the ship even more. The men, strapped to their couch-seats, braced themselves for the splashdown. Three small chutes opened and *Columbia* dipped into the Pacific Ocean, plunging below the surface. Then, like a rubber ball, the ship bobbed up again and rolled about in the pushy waves.

91

Michael Collins photographed LM's upper half "upside down," making its docking approach to the command module. Armstrong and Aldrin are inside. In the background, Earth rises above the moon's horizon.

Apollo had completed the biggest adventure in man's history. At mission control in Houston, a screen pictured Apollo 11's eagle emblem and flashed these words: "Task accomplished . . . July 1969."

Columbia was 950 miles southwest of Hawaii. From 10 miles away, a recovery carrier, the *Hornet*, raced to *Columbia*. In an hour, the astronauts were lifted out and flown by helicopter to the *Hornet*.

The three men had little time to receive the rousing welcome from sailors and from President Nixon, who was aboard. They were rushed into a quarantine trailer and no one except a doctor and a NASA engineer was allowed inside with them. But they could see the President through a trailer window, and could speak with him.

Back in Houston, final medical checkups showed each man to be in perfect health. When they left the LRL after the 21-day quarantine, millions upon millions of Americans greeted them at parades and parties in Houston, New York, Chicago, and Los Angeles.

In Los Angeles, President Nixon gave each astronaut the Medal of Freedom, the highest U.S. civilian award. Armstrong said, "We hope and think that this is the beginning of a new era — the beginning of an era when man understands the universe around him, and the beginning of the era when man understands himself."

"The most exciting thing . . . in the history of science."

The Apollo 11 astronauts finished their mission in a blaze of glory. But for scientists, work had just begun.

The triumphant Apollo 11
astronauts wave to crowds in
New York City.

The time had come to fit together the clues hidden in two
boxes of moon rock and soil. Opening the sealed boxes
was a special thrill.

"As far as I am concerned," said one researcher, "this is
the most exciting thing that has happened in the history
of science."

Moon dust and chips from the 50 pounds of moon
samples were examined under high-powered micro-
scopes. Scientists found that some moon soil samples
consisted of tiny beads of glass — yellow, tan, brown,
dark brown, and clear beads. Large amounts of chro-
mium, titanium, yttrium, and zirconium also were found.

These are "space-age" metals, rare on Earth, and valuable because they withstand great heat without melting. So they can be used to build rockets and jet engine parts.

No sign of water or life, either past or present, was found in the Apollo 11 samples. Nothing was discovered that might endanger life on Earth. Nor did studies of the Apollo 11 samples settle this argument among scientists: Is ours a hot moon, or is it a cold moon?

Hot-moon-scientists were pleased to learn that the Apollo 11 rocks were igneous, or heat-melted, specimens. (Igneous means "formed by fire.") This suggested that the moon had, and might still have, a hot core and active volcanoes and earthquakes. Hot-moon-scientists said lava pouring from volcanoes cooled into igneous rock.

But did the igneous-rock evidence put down the ideas of the cold-moon-scientists? No, the Apollo 11 evidence supported their views, too.

Rocks from Tranquility Base were much older than anyone had expected. Some were as much as 3.5 billion years old — at least as old as the oldest rocks ever found on Earth. They could *not* be rocks from lava flows of only 500 million years ago, as hot-moon-scientists had once believed. In fact, in billions of years, the moon's surface seemed hardly to have changed at all.

Some cold-moon-scientists gave this explanation:

"What we see on the moon's surface today may be scars that formed billions of years ago when the moon, Earth, and the planets were coming into being." The moon, they argued, might have been hot when it formed billions of years back. It cooled — forming igneous rock —

and became a cold, dead world with little or no volcanic action.

Others, who believed the moon was *never* hot, said the heat from meteor crashes could have formed the igneous rock during the moon's early centuries.

But all scientists agreed that the igneous rocks had been formed billions of years ago. "It was as if 99 per cent of the moon's activity took place during the first one per cent of its history," said a geologist.

The cold moon, hot moon debate would go on. To settle it, much more evidence would be needed.

The First Billion Years

Even *older* moon rocks were needed to give clues to what Earth was like in the beginning. This is why:

Although Earth is believed to be about four-and-a-half billion years old — the age of the whole solar system — no Earth rock older than 3.5 billion years of age has ever been found. The first billion years of Earth's history are "missing." On the mountains and highlands of the moon, however, scientists think moon rocks may be four-and-a-half billion years old. Moon explorers to come will collect some of these older rocks. Then, the billion years of creation, missing in Earth's history, might be revealed.

The Apollo 11 rocks and soil were sent to about 140 scientists in the U.S. and in eight other countries. Samples were sliced up, ground into bits, X-rayed, bombarded with radar beams, examined under many kinds of special instruments, studied atom by atom.

The samples put the science spotlight on ideas about the moon's beginnings:

• *The "twin planet" theory.* The moon and Earth may have been formed as "twin planets" from the same whirling gas cloud. Then Earth's pull of gravity turned the moon into a satellite.

• *The "capture" theory.* The moon may have been a planet, a "leftover" body formed long before Earth appeared. In some way, the moon strayed close to the young Earth and was "captured" by it in the early years of the solar system.

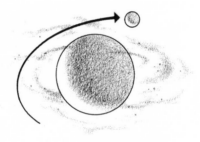

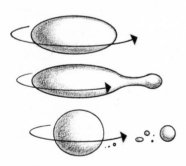

• *The "daughter" theory.* The moon may have been a piece of the Earth, torn from Earth's side in some tremendous upheaval, and flung out into space. (Moon rocks brought back by Apollo 11 are so different from Earth rocks that this theory has been almost ruled out.)

More Clues from the Moon

Meanwhile, the other Apollo 11 experiments were providing information.

The seismometer recorded a severe jolt a day after Armstrong and Aldrin left the moon. If it was the result of a moonquake, it had been a big one. Some scientists argued, however, that the shock might have been caused by a meteorite, or by the seismometer not working properly. However, some day the seismometer might provide clues about whether the moon is hot or cold.

Light beams were bounced off the laser reflector, and astronomers at California's Lick Observatory reported the distance from Tranquility Base to be exactly 226,790.9 miles at one reading. Such laser beam measurements would go on for 10 years.

Scientists were studying the particles captured on the aluminum foil of the solar wind experiment, and also solar wind particles that seem to have been trapped as gases in the moon rocks.

Meanwhile, the public got to see some moon rocks. The first one was put on display in the late summer of 1969 at the Smithsonian Institution, in Washington, D.C. The two-pound rock, solid gray with sharp fragments, was hundreds of millions of years old.

Summing up Apollo 11

Dr. George E. Mueller, head of NASA's manned flight program, summed up the importance of Apollo 11:

"We proved that man is no longer bound to the limit of the planet on which he has lived for so long. . . . We will return to the moon . . . but these are only the first steps. There remains for mankind the task of deciding the next step. . . . The will of the people of this nation and the world will determine whether mankind will make the great leap to the planets."

Moon Bases

APOLLO 11 WAS ONLY the beginning for moon explorers. "We are not going to the moon just to forget about it thereafter," said a NASA official. After the first moon landings more U.S. expeditions were scheduled.

One reason is that Earth's satellite is big. It has an area almost equal to the land mass of North and South America combined. Having touched down on one place for a few hours, men did not know the moon. No one seriously believed that the 50 pounds of soil and rock samples brought back by Apollo 11 would reveal all there was to know about the moon.

Men would have to explore dozens of sites, maybe hundreds. At each site, they would have to dig deeper into layers of moon rock. And they would have to put out more sensitive instruments to record what was happening — on the moon's surface, above it, and far below it.

Sea of Rains

Schröter's Valley ●18

Aristarchus Crater

●17
Marius Crater

●20
Copernicus Crater

Seething Bay

Sea of Vapors

●19
Hyginus Rille

Sea of Serenity

●14

Littrow Crater

Sea of Tranquility

Tranquility Base ●

Sea of Crises

Censorinus Crater

●15

Ocean of Storms

●12

●13
Fra Mauro Crater

Sea of Moisture

Sea of Clouds

Sea of Nectar

Sea of Fertility

●16
Tycho Crater

Soon after Apollo 11 came Apollo 12, in November 1969. Its moon men were Charles Conrad, Jr., commander; Alan L. Bean, pilot of LEM (code-named *Intrepid*); and Richard F. Gordon, Jr., pilot of the command module (*Yankee Clipper*). Conrad and Bean spent 32 hours on the moon's Ocean of Storms. In two walks they collected rocks, set up moonquake and other science

Photo shows original landing sites proposed for Apollo 11 (*flag at Tranquility Base*) through Apollo 20. By early 1970's severe money problems lopped off three of these manned missions. Meanwhile, Russians put unmanned instrument probes on the moon but U. S. decided to study moon and Earth from orbiting "Skylabs" and space stations.

experiments, and gathered in parts of the U. S. *Surveyor 3* probe lying on the moon for 2½ years. Apollo 12 was a solid success.

Apollo 13 in April 1970 was not so fortunate. After an oxygen tank blast on the third day in space, the ship lost much of its oxygen and power supply. However, LEM (*Aquarius*) provided emergency oxygen and emergency power. The men could not land on the moon but did loop around it before returning home in the crippled command ship (*Odyssey*). James A. Lovell, Jr., led Apollo 13; with him were Fred W. Haise, Jr., and John L. Swigert, Jr.

Manned flights to the moon were delayed until early 1971 when Apollo 14 arrived. Its commander was Alan B. Shepard, Jr., America's first man in space. Edgar D. Mitchell piloted LEM (*Antares*), and Stuart A. Roosa handled the command ship (*Kitty Hawk*). Shepard and Mitchell spent 33½ hours on the moon, exploring it in two walks of 4½ hours each. They found big, age-old rocks in the craggy Fra Mauro highlands, set up an atom-run science station, and won high praise from scientists.

Apollo 15 in July 1971 and Apollos 16-17, set for 1972, also were intended to widen man's knowledge of the moon with on-the-spot exploration and expert study.

Next: A Moon Base

After the manned Apollo flights, there remained the possibility that a permanent U. S. scientific outpost might someday be built — the first real moon base.

"We believe we need a moon base as a next step," said a top NASA official. "A base is useful from the standpoint of safety and for men exploring the lunar surface."

101

To help plan the future moon expeditions, NASA hired a retired astronaut, James A. McDivitt, the commander of Apollo 9. In his new job, McDivitt would help select follow-up landing sites and make plans for the moon missions of the 1970's.

Astronauts would begin to stay on the moon for longer and longer periods — if the moon was thought to be worth exploring. Suppose, however, the U.S. Congress did not budget enough money for more manned moon expeditions? NASA would then depend even more on unmanned instrument ships (which you will read about in the next chapter). Or it might build a huge space station in Earth orbit (as you will read in chapter 12), and from this station, men would observe the moon.

The early moon bases would be no more than the LM's that brought the crew. Once on the moon, such LM's would serve as shelter, laboratory, living quarters, radio station, and observatory. They would be slightly larger models of the LM's of Apollo 11 and Apollo 10.

These early LM's, for example, might carry up to 300 pounds of scientific equipment to the moon and bring back up to 100 pounds of rock and soil samples. They would carry enough oxygen to supply the two-man crew for 48 hours.

Later — and larger — LM's would carry up to 700 pounds of equipment and bring back several hundred pounds of rock and soil. And they would carry enough oxygen for at least three full days.

The men would live inside their LM base ships and step out for only short periods, in spacesuits, to collect

"Flying jeeps," such as this proposed design, may carry future moon explorers over the lunar surface.

moon samples and conduct experiments. They would take readings from scientific instruments such as seismometers. The men would ride across the surface in "rover vehicles," to explore craters and mountain foothills. They might also get around by using rocket-powered "flying jeeps."

After three days or so on the moon, the men would rocket back to the command ship orbiting overhead. They would return in the upper half of their LM. In the lower half, left behind on the surface, would be instruments for the next research crew.

The new crew would land near the LM lab and use its instruments along with new ones they had brought along. In this way, little by little men could build a larger

science station. Men could stay on the moon for longer periods, and roam even greater distances across the surface. Unmanned supply ships could bring more oxygen, food, water, equipment, fuel, medicines, and instruments. An unmanned ship loaded with supplies could be sent to a moon site *before* the crew arrived. The ship would not return to Earth and could carry more supplies because it would not be loaded with fuel for a trip home. The crew would land near the supply ship.

In later years, moon explorers might start building a base underground. One such plan called for a football-shaped base on the floor of a wide crater. Men would dig down below the floor, opening up passageways and cave-like rooms for equipment and living quarters. Such an underground base would help protect men from the moon's extreme heat and cold, crashing meteorites, and the intense radiation of the sun.

In underground bases, as many as 30 men could live and work for as long as two years. They would go from one section of the base to the next by walking through pressurized tunnels. To explore the surface, they would wear spacesuits and carry oxygen supplies in back packs.

An observatory with telescopes and other equipment might be built on a platform that could be raised to the surface — or under a "roof" that would slide open to reveal the sky. The absence of a blurring atmosphere on the moon would permit astronomers to see far out into the universe. Some day a base might be built on the moon's far side. This would be useful for radio astronomers, for they would have 2,000 miles of rock — the moon

A LM "taxi" lands near a LM shelter. This is an artist's idea of one step in building a moon base from clusters of special LM's.

itself — shielding them from electrical noises and radio sounds from Earth. This would make it easier to detect sounds coming from distant planets, stars, and galaxies.

Coming: A Colony on the Moon?

With Earth's population growing so quickly, it was no wild dream that human settlers might very well colonize the moon. A base for settlers might be built on the surface with a huge bowl-shaped dome to protect the colony and hold in its oxygen supply.

The first settlers would bring oxygen with them. Later, more would be sent in supply ships. And some day, colonists might be able to produce their own oxygen. Some scientists believe that trapped oxygen could be removed from moon rocks with solar (sun) or atomic energy. And this would cost less than shipping oxygen supplies from Earth.

Settlers would be comfortable inside the domed base, for they would have controlled air pressure. Electricity might be produced with solar or atomic energy. Solar furnaces might melt down moon rock and the melted rock could then be cast into bricks for building.

Men might also use such a furnace to melt water out of permafrost if any lies under the moon's surface. Permafrost is a layer of solidly frozen soil, deep enough under the crust that the sun's heat never reaches it.

In time, a moon colony could thrive and grow. It could become a small town, perhaps a small city. People could raise families on the moon and have useful jobs. They could have many of the comforts of their brothers on

Earth: books, radio and TV, movies, schools, gardens, museums, hospitals, observatories, and so on.

As the 1970's opened, moon bases and even moon colonies seemed to be on the way — scientific bases in the 1970's, colonies perhaps by the 1980's or 1990's.

A wheel-shaped underground moon base of the future. As the cutaway shows, living quarters, medical center, labs, recreation areas, and shops are in the "spokes," farms in the "rim." Above ground: a domed hangar for ferry ships from Earth, and an astronomical observatory.

"For colonists," said NASA's Dr. Thomas O. Paine as he considered the future, "the loneliness would be so lonely, the togetherness so together."

No one knew exactly when the first permanent base would open, or how many settlers might form the first moon colony. Yet this was definite: Some day the moon would be a training ground and a laboratory — perhaps even a home — for men.

The moon would be a stepping stone to the planets.

A test model "rover vehicle" for moon exploration.

Beyond the Moon

WITH THE MOON LANDINGS, man showed he could go deep into space. One big question was: how far? Would man now try to reach the planets?

From the United States, the answer was yes.

"We are looking forward to the days when we will be manning space stations in the sky, conducting moon explorations, and in the distant future, blazing a new trail to the planets." So said NASA official, Dr. Thomas O. Paine, in 1969.

Manned expeditions to the planets will come — but not right way.

First there will be more scouting trips by unmanned instrument ships. In the 1960's, for instance, the U.S. and Russia sent unmanned ships to study Venus and Mars.

NASA ships flew by Venus in 1962, Mars in 1964, Venus again in 1967, Mars again in 1969. Russia penetrated Venus' atmosphere with instruments in 1967 and in 1969.

Instrument ships test a planet's magnetic field and the temperature of its surface and of its upper and lower atmosphere. They report the pressure of the atmosphere and the kinds of gases found in it. They detect water vapor, if any exists. Some ships send TV pictures of planets to Earth. Some gather fresh facts about a planet's moons.

This information helps scientists to judge what forms of life — if any — could survive there; and it provides clues to how and when Earth itself was formed.

In the 1960's much was learned about Mars and Venus. U.S. scientists found that the surface of Mars was more cratered and moon-like than they had believed. Russian scientists discovered that Venus had an extremely dense atmosphere and red-hot rocks on the surface.

In the 1970's the U.S. planned more missions for instrument ships:

One type is the "fly by" mission. The ship makes just one sweep past the planet.

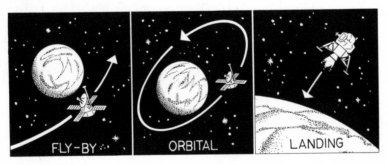

Three Types of Unmanned Mission

Another is the orbiting mission. The ship goes completely around the planet at least once.

A third is the landing mission. The ship tries to land on the planet, or to put instrument capsules down on it.

As you know, the planets in the solar system revolve around the sun. The inner planets, those nearest the sun, are Mercury, Venus, Earth, and Mars. The outer planets are Jupiter, Saturn, Uranus, Neptune, and Pluto. Thousands of small rocks and planets called asteroids also orbit the sun in a broad belt between Mars and Jupiter. They may be the remains of a planet that exploded — or one that never formed into a solid ball.

In the 1970's NASA hoped to send unmanned instrument ships to both the inner planets and the outer planets. Possibly, these unmanned missions would pave the way for manned expeditions — especially to Mars.

Trips to the Inner Planets

These were the unmanned trips planned for the inner planets:

In 1971 two Mariner ships would skim to within a thousand miles of Mars — closer than ever before.

Both ships would orbit Mars for three months or more, measuring the surface temperature, searching out water vapor in the atmosphere, photographing the planet's geographic features, and helping Earth scientists map most of Mars, except for some areas near its north and south poles.

"We can't determine the presence of life with such information," said a U.S. scientist. "But we can try to learn more about Mars as an environment for life." He was, of course, talking about simple forms of life.

In 1973 NASA would send another unmanned mission to Mars in Project Viking. Two ships would orbit Mars, one over the polar regions, one over the equator. Each would drop landing capsules filled with instruments.

The instruments would search for signs of life, test samples of soil and rock pulled back into the capsule, and take readings of surface conditions. All findings would be transmitted to Earth scientists immediately.

Also in 1973, and maybe earlier, NASA would send unmanned ships to fly by Venus and then Mercury. Some scientists say that a few narrow bands of Venus' atmosphere *may* support a simple form of life. But they do not believe that Mercury has life as we know it. The planet is too near the sun. At 770 degrees Fahrenheit, Mercury is hot enough to melt lead.

Reaching the Outer Planets

This was the planning for unmanned trips to outer planets:

Jupiter, Saturn, Uranus, Neptune, Pluto — the distances to these outer planets are tremendous. For example, our moon is some 240,000 miles away. Pluto is at least three billion six hundred million miles away when it is on Earth's side of the sun — *15 thousand times* as far as the moon.

If an astronaut, 30 years old, left for Pluto in a ship powered by a three-stage Saturn V rocket, he would have to travel for 6,000 straight days at 25,000 miles an hour,

112

to reach Pluto. When he arrived, nearly 17 years later, he'd be almost 47 years old.

An unmanned instrument ship, powered by a smaller rocket, would take 40 years to reach Pluto from Earth.

But there *did* seem to be a way to conquer the enormous distances to the outer planets. NASA worked out an ingenious plan to save time and rocket power for such trips. They called it the "Grand Tour of the Planets."

Imagine an instrument ship about to be launched from Kennedy Space Center. The first target is Jupiter, the biggest planet in the solar system. It is big enough to hold 1,300 Earths clustered together. Because of its great size and mass, Jupiter's gravity has a mighty pull. So as the ship nears Jupiter, the pull of gravity sharply boosts the ship's speed, almost as if the giant planet were reeling the ship in. The ship whips around Jupiter, its motion somewhat like that of a ball rushing in and out of a curved *jai-alai* paddle. At the same time, the ship's terrific speed keeps it from crashing into Jupiter, and lets it skim on past.

Now the ship heads for Saturn, from Saturn to Pluto, and from Pluto on out of the solar system.

Along the way, the ship's speed is increased by the gravity pull of each planet that it nears. Each time, the ship darts past the planet and moves on.

A "Grand Tour of the Planets" has two advantages:

Using the power of each planet's gravity to pull the spaceship along, instead of relying only on the ship's rocket power, years of travel time are saved. And of course, it's easier to look over several planets with the

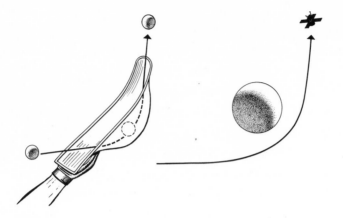

On a "Grand Tour," the pa[th]
of a ship whipping past a
planet is like the path of a
ball whipping in and out [of a]
paddle in a jai-alai game.

same ship, than to send separate ships to each planet.

NASA's dates for tours to the outer planets were 1976-79. Starting in 1976, Jupiter, Saturn, Uranus, Neptune, and Pluto will all be on the same side of the sun. Except for Pluto, all will be in a long, curving row, one behind the other, though millions of miles apart.

This line-up of planets is very rare. The last time the outer planets were lined up this way was in the 1790's, about the time George Washington was President. After 1979 they will not line up this way again for another 180 years, or around the year 2159.

For 1976-79 NASA worked out several possible "Grand Tours" to the outer planets. One flight of two billion eight hundred million miles would go from Earth to Jupiter, Saturn, Uranus, and Neptune. It would take about 10 years, and would not pass Pluto.

A ship making this Grand Tour would start out in September 1977. In 1978 it would pass across the asteroid belt between the orbits of Mars and Jupiter. In

January 1979 the ship would swing by Jupiter. In September 1980 it would pass near the rings of Saturn. Sometime in February 1984, it would come to within 10,000 miles of Uranus. It would move within 15,000 miles of Neptune in November 1986, and then fly right on out of the solar system.

As it passed Neptune, the ship would send back information via radio signals. Although radio signals move so fast they can go around the Earth seven-and-a-half times a second, it would take about eight hours for radio signals to travel from Neptune, more than two-and-a-half billion miles back to Earth.

Through Grand Tour missions, scientists hoped to find answers to such questions about the outer planets as:

Jupiter: What is the Great Red Spot, as big as four

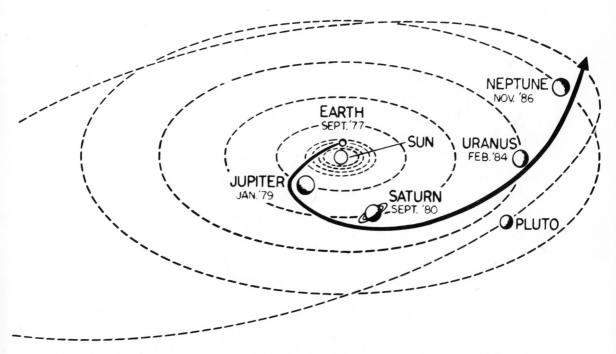

A "Grand Tour of the Planets": An unmanned spacecraft will leave Earth, probably in 1977, and tour the solar system for nine years. The ship's speed will be boosted by each planet's pull of gravity.

Earths, on Jupiter? Why does Jupiter have 12 moons? Does it have a solid surface? What causes the sudden bursts of radio noises coming from Jupiter?

Saturn: Why is Saturn the only planet to have rings? What are they made up of? How wide are they?

Uranus: Does it have a solid surface? Why is it tilted on its axis more than any other planet? What kinds of gases does it have?

Neptune: What lies below the thick gas clouds of Neptune? Why does it have two moons? Might it have more?

Pluto: Why is Pluto more like the inner planets — small, solid, and rocky — than the other outer planets? Was Pluto once one of Neptune's moons? Is Pluto really the outermost planet in the solar system? Is Pluto a "visitor" from the distant reaches of the universe that has been captured by the sun's pull of gravity?

And why are the outer planets different from the inner ones? There is a different material "way out there" in the outer planets — just what is it?

"We need close-up observations to come to grips with these puzzles," said a U.S. scientist. "Exploration of the solar system should be our new goal."

In the 1970's unmanned instrument ships, moving in and out among the planets, would help find answers.

The answers would pave the way for manned flights. Then some day man would go into the far reaches of the solar system — and maybe beyond.

Stations in Space

AFTER APOLLO 11 put the first men on the moon, it became clear that in the early 1970's men would:
- *set up moon bases* for scientific studies (as you read in chapter 10);
- *send out more instrument ships* to gather new facts about distant planets (as you read in chapter 11); and
- *build Earth-orbiting space stations.*

Space stations could open the way for the first manned expedition to another planet – Mars. Some day Mars might be man's biggest base in space! But before that could happen, there was much work to be done.

The Saturn Workshop

By 1972 the U.S. hoped to have its first space station in orbit — a space laboratory, circling the world high over the heads of Earthlings.

Building a laboratory on the ground is one thing — but how do you build a laboratory in space?

With no foundation to build on, and no gravity to hold down the building materials, space station builders had to come up with a new technique: send a piece of the station into orbit, then send other sections into orbit and dock them with the main section.

The first station would be made up of rocket stages and other equipment designed for the Apollo moon project. In one plan, the main part of the space station would be a Saturn rocket stage, fired into orbit and emptied of fuel. Inside the empty rocket would be the walls and floors of a workshop about 50 feet high and about 25 feet across. It was to be called the "Saturn Workshop."

At first, the Saturn Workshop would have a three-man crew. They would live and work in two sections partitioned off by a floor. One section, about one third of the space station, would be the crew's living quarters: kitchen, bathroom, living room, and small bedrooms. A bicycle bolted to the floor with its wheels in mid-air would provide exercise for the weightless crew.

Cots or hammocks would have long zippers to pull up so the men would not float around in the cabin while asleep. During their waking hours, the men would wear shoes with special cleats. The cleats would fit into two-inch openings placed by the thousands over the floor. With a twist of his foot, an astronaut could lock his shoe in place and anchor himself where he stood.

Two thirds of the space station would be a scientific laboratory. There would be no stairway between the

The Saturn Workshop will be divided into living and working quarters.

SATURN

FOOD
PREPARATION

WASTE STORAGE

CREW
QUARTERS

CREW
QUARTERS

EXPERIMENT
WORK AREAS

ENTRY HATCH

laboratory and the living quarters. The men would move back and forth through an opening in the floor by pulling themselves along on a fireman's pole, or by simply "floating" through the opening.

The two-story workshop, unmanned, would be fired into Earth orbit. A command ship carrying the crew would be put into the same orbit. The command ship would catch up with the workshop and dock with it. The three men would stay in the space station for a month. Then they would climb into the command ship, separate it from the workshop, and return to Earth.

Meanwhile, a new command ship and crew would be sent out to link up with and work in the space station for another month. Later, crews might stay in the station for up to 100 days at a time. As many as five ships would be able to dock with the station at the same time.

Why a Space Station?

What could scientists learn in space stations that they could not learn in Earth-based laboratories?

A view of the Earth. From a space station, men can watch Earth spinning below. Each region will come into view again and again. With special instruments and cameras, men can keep watch over croplands, forest areas, oil and mineral deposits, and other natural resources — even schools of fish. By studying cloud formations, they can forecast weather months in advance and help control floods. They can prepare accurate world maps.

A view of space. Astronaut-astronomers will study planets, stars, galaxies, the universe. And they will get much better results, for they will be beyond the shimmering veil of atmosphere — air, gases, vapors, smoke, dirt — that surrounds Earth.

Earth's atmosphere dims, blurs, and absorbs light waves from galaxies, star clusters, stars, comets and other bodies deep in space. Radio waves, X rays, infrared and ultraviolet light are also partly absorbed by the atmosphere — and some of these *never* get through to instruments on Earth's surface. Scientists feel that if they could get outside the atmosphere and gather in all the "radiant energy" waves that come from distant bodies, they might unlock some of the secrets of the universe. Learning the true ages of galaxies and star clusters, for example, would be a key to the puzzle of how and when the universe began.

Weightlessness and man. How long can men be weightless and stay healthy? Even as Apollo astronauts were exploring the moon, scientists were still not sure of the effects on man of being weightless for a long time. If men lived and worked in space stations for several months, or if men took a long trip to Mars or another distant planet, would weightlessness have a bad effect?

The first space station crew would help scientists find out how long men can be weightless and healthy.

After some U.S. space flights, the astronauts had certain small changes in sense of balance, and in bones, blood, muscles, and other body parts. They were not serious. "Such effects disappear in a short time," said space doctors, "but on long flights they might become a problem for the crews." They believed that a kind of "artificial gravity" would have to be created to prevent ailments on long space trips.

Meanwhile, NASA studied how space travel affects living things. It sent a rocket into Earth orbit with frog eggs, plants, insects, and microscopic life aboard. For 45 hours the "passengers" were weightless.

"Plant life reacts far more to weightlessness than animal life," NASA scientists reported. After several hours of weightlessness, for example, the leaves of a pepper plant drooped, twisted, and curled straight down. On Earth, the leaves grew almost straight out and did not sag. Without gravity, scientists said, leaves, stems and roots of plants grew "in unexpected directions."

Other tests were made on bacteria, viruses, and small animals.

And Even Bigger Stations

In 1969 Russia had already built sample space stations. In January, two ships, Soyuz 4 and Soyuz 5, were put into Earth orbit. They docked and two men from Soyuz walked out into space and then climbed into the sister ship to join a third man there. In October, seven men in three ships, Soyuz 6, Soyuz 7, and Soyuz 8, made even more advanced space station tests. These were the first steps toward Russia's goal of building a permanent Earth-orbiting space station.

One Russian plan for the future was to use a huge tank-like structure as a space station core. To enlarge it, four Soyuz-type ships would plug into the core.

Meanwhile, NASA went ahead with America's plans

This proposed space station will house 50 to 100 men with living quarters at the hub and laboratories in the outer areas. Artificial gravity will be created by spinning. In this drawing, delta-winged ferry ships are docked at the base of the hub.

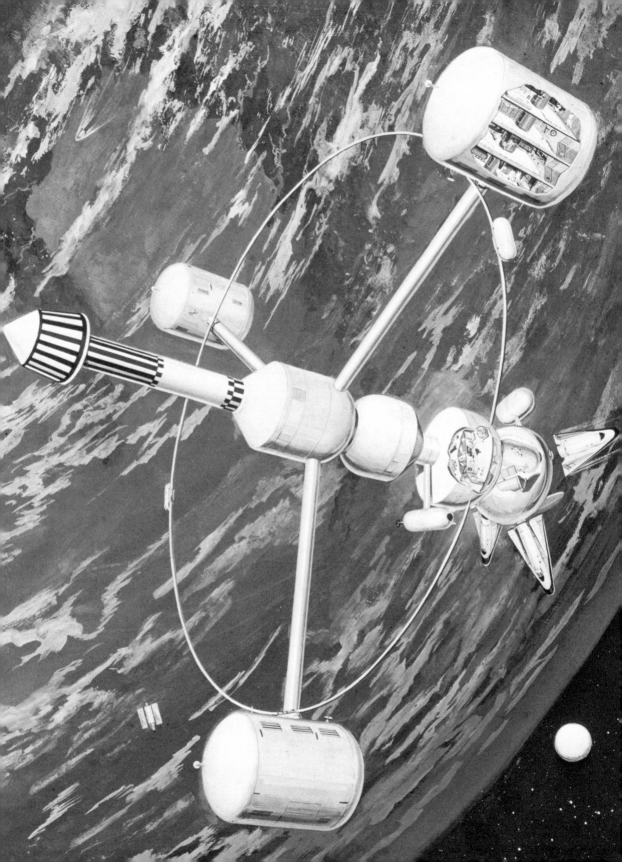

for the big space stations of the future. Colonel Frank Borman, commander of Apollo 8, was chosen to direct the work of designing the large space stations that would come after the Saturn Workshop. These would be ready for year-long Earth orbits by the late 1970's.

Some space stations would be wheel-shaped. Such a station, planned for the late 1970's, would have a central core linked to three outer sections.

The central core would be living quarters for a crew of 12 men. Outer sections, added one by one, would serve as laboratories or as "repair shops" for ships traveling to and from the moon. They could also be jumping-off places for manned flights into deep space.

In time, as the space station expanded, it would hold as many as 100 men for several months at a time. Small ferry-ships would carry crews to and from the station, docking at the base of the central core. Unlike rocket ships, these ferry-ships would not be dumped into the sea after each launch. The little delta-wing ships could glide through Earth's atmosphere and land on a runway.

Another plan called for sending up a station in which the core would be a laboratory, and the outer sections would be living quarters for astronomers, weathermen, conservationists, and other scientists.

By spinning these big stations slowly, about three-and-a-half times a minute, a pull toward the outside and a feeling of gravity would be created for the crew — men not used to space and weightlessness.

"Everyone is not an astronaut," explained a NASA official. "This laboratory would be designed not for astronauts, but for scientists."

124

Mars: Space Station of the Future

Bases on the moon . . . Earth-orbiting space stations . . . Would man one day build a station on Mars?

"Our next big spacecraft program," predicted Dr. Wernher von Braun, a U.S. rocket scientist and a NASA director, "will be manned space stations and laboratories. . . . It appears, too, that the U.S. will have the capability to land a man on Mars by 1982 or 1985. . . ."

After the moon landings, NASA was definitely looking ahead to manned planetary missions. No one expected men to go to *all* the planets. Instrument ships would do that. Besides, so far men knew too little about the planets. For example, scientists are still not certain that Jupiter's surface is solid enough to stand on.

But for a long time, men had thought about exploring one particular planet: Mars — a ball of rock like Earth. The fourth planet from the sun, Mars is 35 million miles from Earth at the nearest point in their orbits. Astronauts could reach Mars in two months — less time than the Pilgrims needed to cross the Atlantic Ocean in 1620.

Of all the planets, after Earth, Mars is the most likely place to find life. The temperature range in places and at times is comfortable enough to support life. No one seriously thinks of finding *intelligent* life on Mars; but there is every chance that the planet does have *simple forms* of life. Some astronomers point to huge dark patches on Mars that change in shape and color. Sometimes the patches seem green, sometimes gray. They could be a sign of simple plant life. Yet other astronomers have never seen these changes.

Until men arrive for a close look, the burning questions about Mars will remain: Is there life, any form of life, on Mars? If so, where and what kind?

"The most dramatic scientific discovery I can imagine during the next 10 years or so would be the discovery of life on Mars." So said Dr. William H. Pickering, a California astronomer. "I believe we will find life there. I think that it will be primitive life — but it will be something."

U.S. plans included an expedition to Mars with two or three ships in convoy formation, under atomic power. A round trip could last nearly two years, allowing many months for exploration and study of the planet.

Besides the questions of life, many other questions about Mars need answers:

What is Mars' atmosphere like?

What is the "bearing" strength of its surface?

How much water and water vapor is there on Mars?

The target date for a landing could be 1982. If men did not touch down on the surface, they would stay in orbit around Mars for observations and send down robots or instruments to gather information for them.

One way or another, men would know Mars.

The daring men who stepped onto the moon in July of 1969 had opened a new chapter in the space age.

Man had broken the bonds of Earth. He had landed on the moon. He would reach Mars. He would reach the distant planets — and perhaps go beyond the solar system.

For space explorers, anything is possible.

Index